P9-DEZ-401

Dry Ice Investigations

Teacher's Guide

Grades 6–8

Skills
Observing, Comparing, Recording, Exploring, Investigating, Working Cooperatively, Communicating, Designing Systematic Observations, Designing Experiments, Logical Thinking, Critical Thinking, Choosing Investigable Questions, Posing Explanations, Asking New Questions, Drawing Conclusions

Concepts
Scientific Inquiry, Properties of Matter, Phases, Phase Change, Sublimation, Particulate Nature of Matter, Interaction of Energy and Matter, Behavior of Gases, Carbon Dioxide

Themes
Matter, Energy, Patterns of Change, Systems and Interactions

Mathematics Strands
Logic and Language, Measurement

Nature of Science and Mathematics
Scientific Community, Science and Technology, Theory-Based and Testable, Cooperative Efforts, Real-Life Applications

by

Jacqueline Barber, Kevin Beals, and **Lincoln Bergman**

LHS GEMS
Great Explorations in Math and Science
Lawrence Hall of Science
University of California at Berkeley

OSSINING PUBLIC LIBRARY

APR 24 2009

Cover Design
Carol Bevilacqua

Cover Photo
Peter Fox

Design and Illustrations
Lisa Klofkorn

Photographs
Richard Hoyt
Laurence Bradley
Peter Fox

Lawrence Hall of Science, University of California,
Berkeley, CA 94720-5200

Chairman: Glenn T. Seaborg
Director: Ian Carmichael

Initial support for the origination and publication of the GEMS series was provided by the A.W. Mellon Foundation and the Carnegie Corporation of New York. Under a grant from the National Science Foundation, GEMS Leader's Workshops have been held across the country. GEMS has also received support from: the McDonnell-Douglas Foundation and the McDonnell-Douglas Employee's Community Fund; Employees Community Fund of Boeing California and the Boeing Corporation; the Hewlett Packard Company; the people at Chevron USA; the William K. Holt Foundation; Join Hands, the Health and Safety Educational Alliance; the Microscopy Society of America (MSA); the Shell Oil Company Foundation; and the Crail-Johnson Foundation. GEMS also gratefully acknowledges the contribution of word processing equipment from Apple Computer, Inc. This support does not imply responsibility for statements or views expressed in publications of the GEMS program. For further information on GEMS leadership opportunities, or to receive a catalog and the *GEMS Network News*, please contact GEMS at the address and phone number below. We also welcome letters to the *GEMS Network News*.

©1999 by The Regents of the University of California. Reprinted, 2001, 2007. All rights reserved. Printed in the United States of America. Student data sheets and other pages intended to be reproduced for students during the activities may be duplicated for classroom and workshop use. All other text may not be reproduced in any form without the express written permission of the copyright holder. For further information, please contact GEMS.

Printed on recycled paper with soy-based inks.

ISBN: 978-0-924886-90-4

COMMENTS WELCOME !

Great Explorations in Math and Science (GEMS) is an ongoing curriculum development project. GEMS guides are revised periodically, to incorporate teacher comments and new approaches. We welcome your criticisms, suggestions, helpful hints, and any anecdotes about your experience presenting GEMS activities. Your suggestions will be reviewed each time a GEMS guide is revised. Please send your comments to: GEMS Revisions, c/o Lawrence Hall of Science, University of California, Berkeley, CA 94720-5200. The phone number is (510) 642-7771 and the fax number is (510) 643-0309. You can also reach us by e-mail at gems@uclink4.berkeley.edu or visit our web site at www.lhsgems.org

Great Explorations in Math and Science (GEMS) Program

The Lawrence Hall of Science (LHS) is a public science center on the University of California at Berkeley campus. LHS offers a full program of activities for the public, including workshops and classes, exhibits, films, lectures, and special events. LHS is also a center for teacher education and curriculum research and development.

Over the years, LHS staff have developed a multitude of activities, assembly programs, classes, and interactive exhibits. These programs have proven to be successful at the Hall and should be useful to schools, other science centers, museums, and community groups. A number of these guided-discovery activities have been published under the Great Explorations in Math and Science (GEMS) title, after an extensive refinement and adaptation process that includes classroom testing of trial versions, modifications to ensure the use of easy-to-obtain materials, with carefully written and edited step-by-step instructions and background information to allow presentation by teachers without special background in mathematics or science.

Staff

Principal Investigator: Glenn T. Seaborg
Director: Jacqueline Barber
Associate Director: Kimi Hosoume
Associate Director/Principal Editor: Lincoln Bergman
Mathematics Curriculum Specialist: Jaine Kopp
GEMS Network Director: Carolyn Willard
GEMS Workshop Coordinator: Laura Tucker
Staff Development Specialists: Lynn Barakos, Katharine Barrett, Kevin Beals, Ellen Blinderman, Beatrice Boffen, Gigi Dornfest, John Erickson, Stan Fukunaga, Philip Gonsalves, Linda Lipner, Karen Ostlund, Debra Sutter
Financial Assistant: Alice Olivier
Distribution Coordinator: Karen Milligan

Workshop Administrator: Terry Cort
Materials Manager: Vivian Tong
Distribution Representative: Felicia Roston
Shipping Assistant: Jodi Harskamp
Director of Marketing and Promotion: Matthew Osborn
Senior Editor: Carl Babcock
Editor: Florence Stone
Principal Publications Coordinator: Kay Fairwell
Art Director: Lisa Haderlie Baker
Senior Artists: Lisa Klofkorn, Carol Bevilacqua, Rose Craig
Staff Assistants: Trina Huynh, Jennifer Lee, Jacqueline Moses, Chastity Pérez, Dorian Traube

Contributing Authors

Jacqueline Barber	Linda De Lucchi	Catherine Halversen	Craig Strang
Katharine Barrett	Gigi Dornfest	Kimi Hosoume	Debra Sutter
Kevin Beals	Jean Echols	Susan Jagoda	Herbert Thier
Lincoln Bergman	John Erickson	Jaine Kopp	Jennifer Meux White
Susan Brady	Philip Gonsalves	Linda Lipner	Carolyn Willard
Beverly Braxton	Jan M. Goodman	Larry Malone	
Kevin Cuff	Alan Gould	Cary I. Sneider	

Reviewers

We would like to thank the following educators who reviewed, tested, or coordinated the reviewing of *Aquatic Habitats* and *Dry Ice Investigations*. Their critical comments and recommendations, based on classroom and schoolwide presentation of these activities nationwide, contributed significantly to this GEMS publication. Their participation in this review process does not necessarily imply endorsement of the GEMS program or responsibility for statements or views expressed. Their role is an invaluable one; feedback is carefully recorded and integrated as appropriate into the publications. **THANK YOU!**

CALIFORNIA

Albany Middle School, Albany
Joanna K. Pace

Longfellow Middle School, Berkeley
Crispin Barrere
Jonathan Cohen
Betty H. Merritt
*Susan Tanisawa

Oxford School, Berkeley
Joe Brulenski
Barbara Edwards
*Janet Levenson
Anne Prozan

School of the Madeleine, Berkeley
Barbara Basinet
Tom Dwyer
Heather Skinner
*Judy Velardi

Stanley Intermediate School, Lafayette
Glenn Hoxie
*Michael Meneghetti
Michael Merrick
Dixie Mohan

Claremont Middle School, Oakland
Susan Cristancho
*Malia Dinell
Courtney Terry
Ann Tingley

Hawthorne School, Oakland
Doug Dohrer
Sonja Ebel
Sonny Kim
*Madeline Lee
Rebecca Marquez

Montclair Elementary School, Oakland
Joe Danielson
Margaret Dunlap
Terry Anne Saugstad
Sheila Sims
Michael Strange
*Sharon Tom

Sherman Elementary School, Oakland
Andrea Mitchell
Marty Price
Jean Rains
*Linda Rogers

Cinnabar School, Petaluma
Judy Bowser
Diana DeMarco

Liberty School, Petaluma
*Fran Korb
Preston Paull

Coronado Elementary School, Richmond
*Jody Anderson
Kevin Eastman
Heidi Garcia
Norah Moore

Edendale Elementary School, San Lorenzo
Terri Kaneko
*Cheryl Tekawa-Pon
Alison Williams

Glen Cove School, Vallejo
Marcia Burnham
Linda Combs
*Cindy Jones
Bruce McDevitt

COLORADO

Cory Elementary, Denver
Carol Calkin
Kay DeLong
*Scott Sala
Debbie Stricker
Margaret Wing

Paonia Middle School, Paonia
Kimber Arsenault
Becky Ruby
*Morrie Rupp
Larry Thompson

ILLINOIS

Williamsville Junior High School, Williamsville
Rhonda Fulks
*Marcie Lane
Julie McPherson
Polly Wise

MASSACHUSETTS

Westfield Middle School, Westfield
Marsha Estelle
Sue Regensberger
*Lisa Strycharz
Sybil Williams

NEW MEXICO

Bernalillo School, Bernalillo
*Belinda Casto-Landolt
Kim Chavez
Sue Fleming
Michelle Mora
Susan Rinaldi
Teresa Whitehead

NEW YORK

Makowski School, Buffalo
Pat Benson
*Sandy Campbell
Sarah Johnson
Dennis Knipfing
Caroline Parrinello

NORTH CAROLINA

Charlotte Latin School, Charlotte
Vicki Carbone
Suzanne Isola

OHIO

Baker Middle School, Marion
Denise Iams
Carol White

PENNSYLVANIA

Sewickley Academy, Sewickley
Bernice Boyle
*Vicki Carbone
Susan Harrison
Dolly Paul
Lori Sherry

TEXAS

Armond Bayou Elementary, Houston
Nancy Butler
Jennifer Chiles
*Myra Luciano
John Ristvey
Lessa Young

Murry Fly Elementary, Odessa
Joy Ellison
Ruben Evaro
Sandra Galindo
*Kym Monacelli
Maria Torres

UTAH

Cook Elementary, Syracuse
*Laurel Bain
Audrey Francis
Natalie Merrill
Kristi Shelley
Liesa Tobler

WASHINGTON

Blue Heron Middle School, Port Townsend
Ted Davis

Challenger Elementary, Issaquah
*Roberta Andresen
Kathy Caravano
Bonnie Cole
Joyce Neufeld

* Trial test coordinators

Acknowledgments

This guide owes its multilayered richness to a large number of talented people who contributed to it during a somewhat longer process of gestation than the "normal" GEMS guide.

The first glimmers of this guide came about when one of the authors was inadvertently stuck in an outreach situation missing crucial materials to teach a scheduled lesson. He did happen to have dry ice, however, and grabbed some other materials for his students to begin investigating it. The episode proved so exciting it inspired an LHS class on gases, which emphasized discovery. Former LHS Chemistry Department Director Laura Lowell helped develop this class during its early stages.

The wise counsel of former GEMS Science Curriculum Specialist Cary Sneider must be acknowledged. Cary, who served on the Contents Working Group for the *National Science Education Standards,* was crucial in improving our understanding of the emphasis on inquiry in the *National Science Education Standards* and in widening the idea of inquiry beyond narrow definitions of controlled experimentation.

We were also fortunate to have this unit reviewed by Israeli scholar Varda Bar, an internationally recognized educational researcher whose work relates to student ability to acquire key scientific concepts, including concepts relating to gravity, air, and evaporation. In particular, she made important suggestions concerning our presentation of the particulate nature of matter.

As described in "Behind the Scenes," our work on this unit was also assisted by Anthony Cody, an Oakland teacher who has worked with LHS educational programs and whose master's thesis focuses on how best to develop inquiry abilities and understandings in students, including some dry ice activities. In addition to his thesis, we also benefited greatly from conversations and e-mail exchanges with him as the unit developed.

The teachers who helped us trial-test this unit locally and nationally are listed at the front of the guide. Their dedicated efforts, and the involvement of their students, make GEMS what it is! Several must be especially acknowledged. Jonathan Cohen, a teacher at Longfellow Middle School in Berkeley, developed an inquiry-related student worksheet that influenced our own student sheets. His worksheet has been used as an instructive example for other teachers in GEMS professional development institutes. He, along with Vicki Carbone and Suzanne Isola of Charlotte Latin School in Charlotte, North Carolina, and Denise Iams and Carol White of Baker Middle School in Marion, Ohio, took part in a "mini-trial-test" of the final unit which helped us immensely. Ted Davis and Laura Tucker, the GEMS Workshop Coordinator, took part in this final test effort as well, presenting the unit to five middle school classes in Port Townsend, Washington, and providing detailed comment.

We are also indebted to Karen Ostlund, the GEMS Texas Nexus Coordinator, and Steve Rakow, long time GEMS Associate and NSTA 1998–1999 President, for their cogent and detailed comment on this unit especially regarding experimentation.

As the guide was being developed, LHS Director Dr. Ian Carmichael initiated a "Hall Fellow" visiting scholar program that brought us the chemistry expertise and research abilities of Deborah Hall. She did extensive research on chemistry misconceptions, commented on many aspects of the unit, and made suggestions for the chemistry content in the "Behind the Scenes" background section.

The "Behind the Scenes" baton was then passed to Jennifer G. Loeser, a staff member of the LHS Living By Chemistry program, who synthesized a great deal of chemistry knowledge to provide an initial draft which was then edited and revised by the authors. U.C. Berkeley Chemistry Professor Angy Stacy, who is the Principal Investigator for Living by Chemistry, and its Director Jennifer Claesgens also assisted us in the development and review of these activities.

Contents

Introduction

This unit revolves around the intriguing nature of dry ice and the incessant curiosity it provokes in all those who have the opportunity to interact with it. Whenever science (especially chemistry) is depicted on film or television, you can almost guarantee that you'll see dry ice bubbling away in a colorful liquid. Music videos, scary movies, theatrical plays, and Halloween frequently feature its eerie heavy fog slowly and silently creeping across a surface. Although it is perhaps the ultimate symbol of "fun science," students rarely have the opportunity to explore it themselves in science classes, most likely because many teachers often don't know where to get it, don't know what to do with it, and are intimidated by safety issues. This guide hopes to deal thoroughly with all these issues, and to build upon the wondrous appeal of dry ice to provide a highly memorable and powerful science learning experience. Brace yourself for excitement!

Dry ice is actually the solid form of carbon dioxide (CO_2), and it behaves in fascinating and unexpected ways. It also has many uses in daily life, especially in various methods of refrigeration, fire extinguishers, and new industrial cleaning methods. Our experience has shown that there is nothing quite like dry ice investigations to make students' eyes and minds' pop wide open. **In this unit, your students have the opportunity to investigate this unique substance, its behaviors, and its interactions with a variety of common materials, while learning more about the history and nature of science, and the nature of matter at both the visible and invisible levels.**

This unit has three intertwined content strands—each enhanced by the others:

> **Scientist's Mindset**—Students are thrust into the shoes of scientists as they are challenged to explore dry ice as if they are seeing it for the very first time. **Students are asked to make no assumptions, encouraged to wonder why, and supported in coming up with their own explanations for phenomena they observe.** Simultaneously, they learn about the work of early scientists in finding out about the nature of matter. They learn how key scientific discoveries have been made when scientists questioned what others thought, even when it was unpopular. The scientific motto of London's Royal Society, *Nullius in verba,* (loosely translated as "don't take anybody's word for it—see for

yourself") comes to life as students explore dry ice and wonder why it behaves as it does. The curiosity and sense of discovery is almost palpable in the classroom.

Tackling Key Concepts in Chemistry—Numerous physical phenomena present themselves through dry ice—from the nature of gases, to the quirks of phase change, condensation, and the many other ways that matter and energy interact. The research literature shows that most students' and even adults' understandings of these physical phenomena are fraught with misconceptions. There's no better time to help students construct a more solid understanding of some of these key concepts than when they are engaged in first-hand interaction with the phenomena, wondering why, and coming up with their own explanations. While it is tempting to try and "teach it all," true conceptual change comes from deeper and more meaningful engagement with these concepts where the learner is given the opportunity to see the problems with their existing (incorrect) explanations. **Thus, we have chosen to introduce students to a model for understanding how energy can change properties of matter—the kinetic molecular theory.** This involves having students grapple with the foundational concepts of the particulate nature of matter, without which one cannot truly understand many physical phenomena, including phase change. It is our hope that this will help students begin to construct a basic working model which can serve as a foundation to future learning about the nature of matter.

Guided Preparation for Open Inquiry—Students' driving curiosity about dry ice makes it an ideal topic on which to focus student-led open-ended inquiry (where students choose a question they are interested in and plan and conduct their own investigation to answer that question). The importance of including these "full inquiry" experiences in the science curriculum is recognized and described by the *National Science Education Standards* and is key to preparing learners to own the process of finding out about the world. However, as experienced teachers know, students need a great deal of preparation to be able to get past the exploration phase and effectively design and conduct investigations. In designing this unit, attempts were made to provide a progression of more and more sophisticated ways to find out and to carefully tease apart the individual skills that students need in order

See the "Behind the Scenes" section on page 133 for a review of students' common early conceptions of these physical phenomena.

Be sure to read the special section on page 10 entitled "Using Dry Ice Investigations to Help Your Students Conduct Open-Ended Investigations." It provides important information that will help you make powerful and effective use of this unit and enable your students to engage in "full inquiry," as recommended by the National Science Education Standards.

to successfully conduct their own open-ended investigations. **Most of the unit focuses on the guided inquiry experiences that provide the "scaffolding" to support students in becoming independent inquirers. The culmination of the unit involves students in choosing an investigable question, and planning and conducting an investigation to answer their question.** While many students may have mastered some of the individual skills that are promoted through the guided inquiry section of the guide, we have included experiences to prepare students for skills they aren't typically taught, for instance choosing investigable questions and deciding what kind of an investigation path to choose (a systematic observation or an experiment). *Dry Ice Investigations* models the use of good plans, provides opportunities for students to make plans, provides a structure for planning, and allows opportunities to revise plans.

While any one of these three strands would be a sufficient challenge for students, it was felt that the opportunity was too rich to forego the inclusion of any one strand. Teachers may choose to amplify one or more, or to delve more deeply into particular aspects, to align with their own curricular goals.

For some suggestions about how to tailor the unit to suit the needs of your students, see "Choosing a Pathway Through Dry Ice Investigations," *on page 12. The chart on page 13 provides a more visual sense of how these three main content strands weave throughout the unit.*

Session-by-Session Overview

Dry Ice Investigations is an 11-session unit. **Activity 1** requires three sessions to present. It focuses on setting up the expectations for the scientific habits of mind of objective observation, wondering why, making no assumptions, and posing explanations. Students are presented with historical information about early scientists and introduced to a model for understanding how energy can change properties of matter.

In Session 1, students hone their observation skills as they play a game in which the challenge is to describe something as though they were an extraterrestrial viewing the object for the first time.

In Session 2, students make detailed observations of an ordinary ice cube and then a piece of dry ice, making comparisons between the two substances. The teacher does a demonstration in which energy (heat) is added to each piece of ice.

In Session 3, students are presented with a particulate model of matter and asked to apply this model to their understanding of what happened in the demonstration when water and dry ice were placed on the hot plate.

Activity 2 is a three-session activity in which students are guided through the processes of exploration and systematic observation as ways of finding out. They learn the characteristics of systematic observation and its advantages as compared to exploration as a way of answering questions. They are introduced to the language and system of phases and phase change at both the macro and microscopic levels.

In Session 1, students are given a collection of materials with which to explore dry ice in an open-ended way.

In Session 2, students are guided through a more systematic observation of a phenomenon, as they investigate what happens when you put dry ice in soap solution. Through this systematic observation, they discover that dry ice changes directly from solid to gas, and revisit the molecular model as a way to further understand how energy and matter interact.

In Session 3, students attempt to solve the mystery of the floating bubbles as they use their new-found knowledge about dry ice to explain why soap bubbles float in a container of dry ice. They practice using systematic observation as a way of answering a question and then plan another systematic observation as a way to confirm their tentative explanation.

Activity 3 is a one-session activity in which students are guided through conducting an experiment. Students distinguish between systematic observation and experiments and are introduced to the concepts of test and outcome variables. They discover that increased energy (temperature) increases the rate of sublimation of the dry ice.

In Session 1, students do a variation of the systematic observation they conducted to find out what happens when dry ice is placed in a soap solution. But this time they transform it into an experiment, with a comparison group, and controlled variables. They do the experiment once, answering the question, "Does temperature affect the rate at which dry ice sublimates?" Then they do the experiment again, this time coming up with a quantifiable outcome variable.

Activity 4 includes four sessions in which students plan and conduct their own investigations in an open-ended way. The teacher provides the "scaffolding" to assist students in planning successful investigations, helping them gain experience in distinguishing between investigable questions and non-investigable questions as well as choosing what investigation path to take.

In Session 1, pairs of students participate in a question-categorizing activity and then choose their own investigable questions and the kind of investigation they plan to design.

In Session 2, students complete their investigation plan for either a systematic observation or an experiment.

In Session 3, students conduct their investigations, refine them as necessary, and then conduct them once again (or a follow-up investigation, as appropriate).

In Session 4, students share the results of their investigations with others.

Assessment Suggestions and Literature Connections

Dry Ice Investigations, like all GEMS guides, includes special sections on assessment and literature connections. The "Assessment Suggestions" section outlines selected student learning outcomes, describes ways that assessment tasks are built into these activities, and lists additional assessment ideas. The "Literature Connections" section highlights books that make strong connections to the learning in these activities. We welcome your suggestions.

"Summary Outlines," including detailed preparation checklists in the "Getting Ready" sections, are provided to assist you in preparing and presenting the activities. Additional, removable copies of student data sheets are also included. A "Behind the Scenes" background section is intended to assist you in considering questions students may have.

Important Comment about Using Dry Ice in the Classroom

There are some challenges involved with obtaining and maintaining a supply of dry ice and ensuring its safe use, as you will read in the next section. It is worth saying that we heard over and over from teachers who trial tested the unit, that the preparation and care necessary were well worth the extra effort.

Conclusion

It is our hope that *Dry Ice Investigations* will communicate that science is not about a step-by-step procedure. It's about wondering why, asking questions, observing, coming up with possible explanations, and then designing investigations to test those explanations and come up with more questions, investigations, and explanations! This is not different from the "real" scientific world, in which scientists wonder why, ask questions, come up with possible explanations and then revise those explanations as they learn more. Great scientists are not different from other great learners—they need to be open to changing their explanations and understandings based on the new data they learn.

With this GEMS unit, we hope you and your class share a "sublime" scientific experience!

A Sublime Semantic Note: When dry ice transforms from a solid into a gas without going through the liquid phase, the process is called "sublimation." The verbs "sublimate" and "sublime" are both used to refer to this process. We use the two interchangably in the text, depending on the syntax of the sentence and author/editorial preference. Both are correct. The use of "sublimate" has the advantage of more directly echoing the process of "sublimation."

Obtaining and Maintaining Dry Ice

Where do you get dry ice? There are a number of local outlets for dry ice in most regions of the United States, and some that will even ship dry ice to you. (See the "Resources" section on page 156.) Dry ice is frequently used for transporting perishables, and can often be found in the yellow pages (under "Dry Ice"). Look also in the yellow pages under the heading "Gas–Industrial" for more sources. Dry ice is also available at quite a few retail grocery, convenience, and liquor outlets. You may even be able to get a grocery store to donate it to your worthy cause. Some scientific laboratories have dry ice makers, and are happy to provide teachers with all they need free of charge. If there is a university or other science research facility in your community, start with a call to the physics department.

How much will I need? Six of the eleven sessions in this unit require dry ice (see "Time Frame" on page 14 for information on which sessions). Dry ice is typically sold in "blocks" for a cost of about $15. One block usually consists of four dry ice "slabs" (each about 12" square and 2" thick) though this can vary. Some companies are now selling dry ice in pellet form. Any form will work. In general, each session needing dry ice can be done with one slab of dry ice (or less)—if you encourage your students to use it sparingly. Students can discover just as much using small amounts, and their investigations tend to be more carefully constructed when there is less dry ice available—but firm teacher-imposed limits are needed to enforce this! Thus, **one or two blocks (4–8 slabs) should be plenty for one class of 32 students to complete the entire unit.** The relatively wide range depends upon: a) how far apart you schedule the various sessions that need dry ice; b) how well you store the dry ice (thereby limiting loss); and c) how successful you are at encouraging teams to use small amounts of dry ice.

What's the best plan for obtaining and maintaining the dry ice? There are two approaches you can take to obtaining and maintaining dry ice: 1) get the amount of dry ice you need each day; or 2) obtain enough dry ice for several days at a time, and find a way to keep it frozen. The method you choose should depend on whether it is easier for you to *obtain* the dry ice, or easier for you to *maintain* it.

> **Strategy 1: Obtaining dry ice daily.** If there is a convenience store which sells dry ice located right on your way to school, you might choose just to pick up the

amount you need for that day. If your source is not so conveniently located and/or is not open during hours that are convenient for you, you might want to ask someone else to help out. Obtaining and delivering dry ice to the school is a perfect task for a parent volunteer. Students treat the "dry-ice delivery person" like a hero!

Strategy 2: Obtaining enough dry ice for several days at a time. The challenge of maintaining dry ice is keeping it from subliming (turning from solid into gas) before you are ready to use it. Scientific supply companies sell relatively inexpensive "dry ice keepers." (See the "Resources" section on page 156.) These are basically large styrofoam boxes with very thick walls (about 3"), and are usually effective in keeping dry ice for about 3 days. Especially if you are planning to do this unit in the future, it might be worth investing in one of these. There are many other jerry-rigged systems that can work just as well. Some teachers have wrapped dry ice with thick layers of newspapers, old blankets, thermal blankets, or other insulating materials, then placed the whole thing in a large cooler. Caution: the cooler should **not** be an airtight one. If it is, simply leave the latch open. Better yet, construct your own "dry ice keeper" by lining a large box (at least 2 feet square) with styrofoam (at least 1" thick). (One teacher took a saw to old kick boards!) The larger the volume of dry ice, the longer it will keep. **Do not put dry ice in a refrigerator or freezer.**

Important Safety Information About Dry Ice

Before you learn more about the activities in this unit, there are three important things about dry ice you need to know:

1) Dry ice is extremely cold. If touched briefly it is harmless, but prolonged contact will "burn" the skin (destroy skin cells). Although it is important that safety precautions be stressed early and often with students, in eight years of teaching this unit to thousands of students we have never had a reported injury. Students are required to not touch dry ice with their skin, but are encouraged to handle it with spoons, tweezers, or leather gloves. **It is important to be strict with these parameters, and to let students know that if they are unable to abide by these precautions, they**

cannot take part in the activities. (And they *will* want to take part, we can assure you!!!)

2) Dry ice *sublimes* or *(sublimates)*—it turns directly from a solid into carbon dioxide gas. If stored in an airtight container, it may cause the container to burst as it expands into a gas. For this reason: Do not put dry ice in containers with screw tops or other airtight seals, unless the seal is flexible, as in putting a balloon over the mouth of a vial, or the seal of a ziplock bag. Do not allow students to seal a container with a finger for any length of time. Do not store it for any amount of time in an airtight glass container.

3) Carbon dioxide gas is colorless and odorless—if too much accumulates in an unventilated space, it can reduce the amount of oxygen available. For this reason, do not store dry ice in a small, unventilated room. If transporting dry ice in your car, be sure to keep a window cracked to allow CO_2 gas to escape.

Using *Dry Ice Investigations* to Help Your Students Conduct Open-Ended Investigations

The Truth About "The Scientific Method"

Over the past century, students (including most of us who are now teaching science!) have learned about "The Scientific Method." While described in slightly different ways by different teachers over time, students have generally been taught that there is a rigid, linear, step-by-step process that scientists use to find out about the natural world. This misrepresents science. (See pages 121 and 144 of the *National Science Education Standards*, developed in 1996 by the National Research Council.)

In fact, scientists use a variety of scientific methods (note the plural). These scientific methods, perhaps better described as **scientific inquiry methods**, provide a repertoire of strategies that can be brought to bear in a logical progression to find out more about a situation. Many people are surprised to learn that scientists don't just conduct **controlled experiments** (a comparison between two situations that are alike in all ways but one), but also, when appropriate, conduct **systematic observations** (observing a situation with planned conditions over time) or combine a variety of other approaches, depending on the circumstances.

Although the classic scientific method sequence (beginning with question, hypothesis, experimental design, etc.) does represent a summary of key phases of a scientific investigation, it is not uncommon for a scientist to go back and forth between two phases (or inquiry methods) before proceeding to the next. So, for instance, a scientist rarely arrives at a question without having had the opportunity to first explore and observe the subject of study. Often a scientist will refine a preliminary question by again exploring with materials. Likewise, meaningful hypotheses come from having had some firsthand experience interacting with the situation. In addition, designing an experiment is nearly always preceded by running some pilot studies, in order to try out and refine procedures, identify variables, devise ways to control variables, and come up with ways to measure the test variable.

What was once called, "The Scientific Method," is now called the inquiry process. The process of inquiry is a flexible and dynamic process that includes more than just conducting controlled experiments.

Helping Students Move Beyond Natural Inquiry

Children inquire naturally. They are in fact experts at the process of exploration and rarely need guidance in inquiring in this free form way. However, moving to more systematic ways of inquiring, such as conducting a systematic observation or a controlled experiment, is something that needs to be learned and usually requires a fair amount of guidance. The *National Science Education Standards* call for students to be given opportunities to engage in **partial inquiry** (also called **guided inquiry**) in which they develop abilities and understanding of selected aspects of the inquiry process. The standards also say that students should be provided with opportunities to engage in **full inquiry** (also called **open-ended inquiry**) in which students choose a question, design an investigation, gather evidence, formulate an answer to the original question, and communicate the investigative process and results.

Allowing students to conduct open-ended inquiry is uncommon in most classrooms. When students *are* given the opportunity, they are typically thrown into the situation with little more than a worksheet describing, "The Scientific Method" and perhaps some practice in setting up controlled experiments. This is not enough. Students need to know that there are more ways to investigate than just controlled experiments. They need practice in choosing and refining investigable questions, selecting an appropriate pathway to answer their question, in identifying possible variables, and quantifying outcome variables. They need practice in putting all the aspects of inquiry together. Without this guidance and practice, students often choose questions that can't be answered experimentally. They likewise may choose inappropriate ways to answer questions, have no way to quantify their evidence, and draw conclusions unrelated to the evidence. The result is often frustrating to students and teachers alike. Most often, students' abilities to inquire don't enable them to be more systematic or productive—and to move beyond exploration (which, as we've said, they already do quite well without instruction). And there are some who believe that forcing students through a rigid and linear process even impairs their natural born ability to inquire!

There is a huge need for instructional materials that support and guide students in being able to inquire independently—that is precisely what this unit seeks to do. *Dry Ice Investigations* provides students with **a sequence of guided-inquiry opportunities that prepare them to successfully conduct their own open-ended investigations**—which is the culmination of the unit. Depending on your students' prior experience, they may be able to skip some of the guided sequence, or they may need more practice and guidance in some areas. *Dry Ice Investigations* is designed as a flexible tool for you to use to help your students learn to engage in open-ended inquiry.

On the next two pages, please see "Choosing a Pathway through *Dry Ice Investigations*" with a chart that depicts the main strands of the unit. Looking over the suggestions there should give you some ideas about how to make a plan on how best to use this unit effectively and flexibly to meet the needs of your students.

Choosing a Pathway
through *Dry Ice Investigations*

Dry Ice Investigations is designed to be a flexible instructional tool. The entire 11-session unit will provide students with three intertwined content strands: one related to **chemistry concepts,** one related to instilling a **scientist's mindset,** and one related to **conducting investigations.**

While the sequence of activities in the unit has been carefully designed to interrelate for a rich learning experience of all three strands, a teacher might choose to spend more or less time on a particular part of the unit depending on the prior experience of the class.

While all three strands are present in all activities as part of the student experiences, the emphasis of the **explicit instruction** related to each strand can be mapped out as shown on the chart on the facing page.

So, for example, if your students have had a lot of experience in making careful and objective observations, you might want to skip or shorten Activity 1, Session 1.

Students who have had lots of experience designing experiments and quantifying outcome variables might skip or shorten Activity 3, Session 1.

There may be classes who don't need the amount of planning time in Activity 4 or who might spend less time on the description of the particulate nature of matter (portions of Activity 1 and Activity 2).

On the other hand, you might decide to amplify the amount of time you spend in one part of the unit, if you find that your students need more exposure to a particular concept represented there.

If you are considering shortening or excerpting a session, we suggest that you read the session first before making a final decision, as most sessions contain multiple elements related to more than one of the three main strands.

Emphasis of Explicit Instruction in *Dry Ice Investigations*

	Activity 1			Activity 2			Activity 3	Activity 4			
	Session 1	Session 2	Session 3	Session 1	Session 2	Session 3	Session 1	Session 1	Session 2	Session 3	Session 4
CHEMISTRY CONCEPTS			particulate nature of matter, matter and energy		kinetic molecular theory, phases, phase change, sublimation	gases					
SCIENTIST'S MINDSET	objective observation	observation, explanation, wondering	explanation, wondering, revising explanations	observation, explanation, wondering	observation, explanation, wondering, revising explanations	observation, explanation, wondering, revising explanations					
GUIDED PREPARATION FOR OPEN INQUIRY				exploration	systematic observation	systematic observation	experimenting, quantifying outcome variable	distinguishing investigable questions, choosing correct investigation method	planning the investigation	conduct investigations	communicate about investigations

© 1999 by The Regents of the University of California, LHS-GEMS. *Dry Ice Investigations*. **May be duplicated for classroom use.**

Time Frame

Activity 1: Scientist's Mindset

Activity 2: Systematic Observation

Activity 3: Experimenting

Activity 4: Conducting Dry Ice Investigations

* These sessions require dry ice.

What You Need for the Whole Unit

The quantities below are based on a class size of 32 students. Depending on the number of students in your class, you may, of course, need different amounts of materials.

This list gives you a concise "shopping list" for the entire unit. Please refer to the "Getting Ready" sections for each activity. They contain more specific information about the materials needed for the class and for each team of students.

Non-Consumables

- ❏ a pencil, ruler, or other easily accessible object to model making observations
- ❏ a pair of plastic-handled adult scissors or another object to serve as the mystery object you describe to the class
- ❏ small insulated container for storing pulverized dry ice
- ❏ hammer
- ❏ 2 cloths (old T-shirts or T-shirt sized rags)
- ❏ 1 hot plate or electric skillet
- ❏ 1 extension cord (if needed for hot plate or overhead projector)
- ❏ 1 leather work glove (for the teacher to wear)
- ❏ 6–8 plastic cups with regular ice cube
- ❏ 6–8 plastic cups with dry ice
- ❏ 3 plastic Petri dishes (about 4" in diameter)
- ❏ a handful of BBs
- ❏ overhead projector
- ❏ 1 cold water dispenser, such as a dishtub or cooler (or access to a sink)
- ❏ 1 hot water dispenser (such as an electric coffee maker)
- ❏ 16 trays
- ❏ 12–16 tweezers
- ❏ 48–96 clear plastic cups
- ❏ 6–16 cups that will not melt with hot water in them (such as heavy plastic or styrofoam)
- ❏ 12–16 medicine droppers
- ❏ 12–24 plastic spoons (or 32 leather gloves)
- ❏ 12–16 small plastic flasks or vials (without lids)
- ❏ 12–16 pennies or other metal objects
- ❏ 1 high-sided transparent container, such as an empty aquarium or a large (5 gallon) heavy-duty glass cylindrical container

An overhead transparency of each of the following:

❑ Atoms in History (master on page 45)
❑ Molecular Diagram of a Solid (master on page 46)
❑ Energy and Matter Questionnaire (master on page 47)
❑ Phase Change Diagram A (master on page 72)
❑ Phase Change Diagram B (master on page 73)
❑ Planning Our Investigation (first page only; master on page 108)
❑ Sorting Questions 1 (master on page 112)
❑ Sorting Questions 2 (master on page 113)
❑ Question Strips (front side only; master on page 114)
❑ Investigation Rubric (master on page 126)

Optional:
❑ 1 flat piece of metal to place on top of a burner or skillet with high sides

Consumables

❑ ice cubes (one ice cube per team of 4–6 students)
❑ 1 or 2 blocks of dry ice (See "Obtaining and Maintaining Dry Ice" on page 7 for more information.)
❑ 1 box of ziplock sandwich bags
❑ 1 box of drinking straws
❑ 12–16 balloons (9" or 12" balloons both work well)
❑ 6–8 ziplock sandwich bags
❑ dishwashing soap
❑ cup with very small amount of bubble solution or diluted liquid dishwashing soap (approximately 2 tablespoons of soap in 1 cup of water)
❑ about 5 straws or a few bubble blowers
❑ matches
❑ a cup of hot water
❑ material needed for Activity 4, Session 3—as indicated by student groups

Copies of the following:
❑ 32 Scientific Journals (masters at back of guide)
or
32 each of the following student sheets:
__ Notes from an Extraterrestrial (master on page 25)
__ As if Seeing It for the First Time (master on page 34)
__ Comparing Substances (master on page 35)
__ Adding Energy (master on page 36)
__ Energy and Matter Questionnaire (master on page 47)
__ Dry Ice Explorations (master on pages 58–61)

___ Marge's Systematic Observation (master on page 71)

___ Mystery of the Floating Bubbles (master on page 80)

___ Marge's Experiment: Take 1 (master on page 90)

___ Marge's Experiment: Take 2 (master on page 91)

___ Materials List (master on page 120)

___ Our Dry Ice Investigation (master on pages 121–122)

___ Follow-Up Investigation (master on page 127)

and

16 each of the following student sheets:

___ Planning Our Investigation (master on pages 108–111)

___ Sorting Questions 1 (master on page 112)

___ Sorting Questions 2 (master on page 113)

___ the two-sided Question Strips (masters on pages 114–115)

___ Systematic Observation or Experiment? (master on page 116)

Optional:

❑ newspapers to cover work surface

❑ 6 Dry Ice Challenges (master on page 62)

❑ 32 copies each of Phase Change Diagrams A and B (masters on pages 72–73) for students to add to their Scientific Journals

General Supplies

❑ 32 pencils

❑ 7–8 pieces of butcher paper

❑ 1 marker

❑ masking tape

❑ glue

❑ an overhead pen

❑ 16 envelopes

Optional:

❑ 32 file folders for the Scientific Journal pages

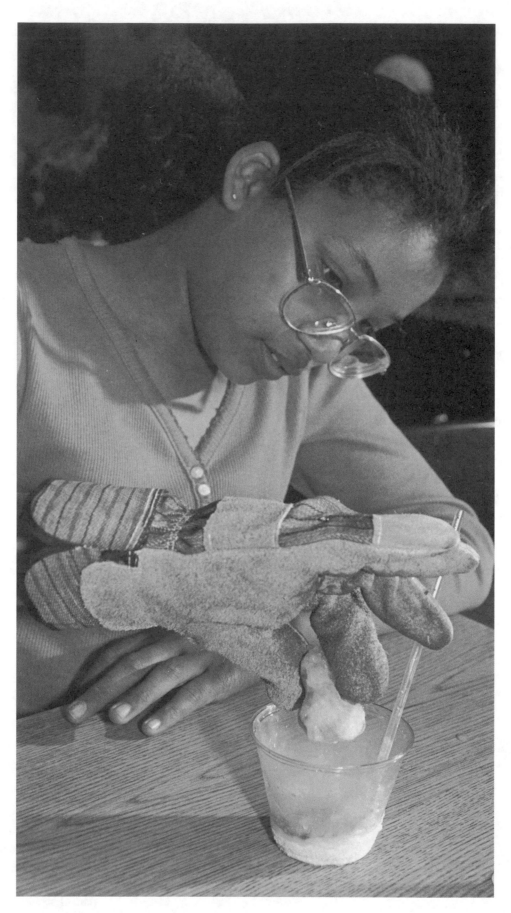

Activity 1: Scientist's Mindset

Overview

In this three-session activity, students take on the role of scientists, as they begin learning about dry ice. In Sessions 1 and 2, students practice making objective observations and comparisons and seeing and thinking for themselves. They play an observation game in which they are challenged to objectively describe a variety of objects. Then they observe and compare water ice and dry ice. Students are encouraged to cast out all prior assumptions, and see things with fresh eyes. They are encouraged to ask questions and come up with their own explanations, even explanations that may seem "wild." They are told that many of the greatest scientists in history came up with ideas and explanations that were at first considered "stupid" or wrong, but their willingness to see and think for themselves led to great discoveries.

In Session 3, students learn something that seems pretty "wild." Many years ago, scientists did careful observations and came up with an explanation (or model) to explain how matter behaves. They proposed the idea that all matter is composed of tiny, moving, particles, called molecules. Years later, this model still fits what we now know. Scientists are still conducting experiments to improve and refine our explanations for how matter behaves. Students are presented with this particulate model and then given the opportunity to apply the model to explain their experiences with water ice and dry ice thus far.

The objectives of this activity are to: provide students with experience making objective observations and comparisons; encourage students to take on a scientist's mindset by wondering why and making no prior assumptions; communicate that good scientists (and good thinkers!) constantly revise their explanations based on new data; introduce the concept that heating causes changes in properties of materials; elicit preconceptions of the particulate nature of matter; identify water ice as H_2O and dry ice as CO_2; and introduce a model for understanding how energy can change properties of matter (the kinetic molecular theory).

Encouraging students to come up with their own ideas is emphasized because we've found that some students are reluctant to attempt explanations, and are overly concerned about knowing the "right answer." Urging students to work with their own observations and ideas also serves an equalizer, encouraging full participation.

Of course everybody makes assumptions—it's impossible not to, and not even desirable! Sometimes those assumptions help us think, as we come up with hypotheses and explanations. Sometimes they get in the way of our thinking, as we get stuck and only "see" things that are consistent with our assumptions (which may be incorrect!). It's ideal to be aware of our assumptions. Asking students to "make no assumptions" helps them use fresher, unjaded eyes and minds as they embark on their scientific inquiries.

Session 1: Introduction to Observing

In this session, students hone their observation skills as they play a game in which the challenge is to describe something as though they were an extraterrestrial seeing the object for the first time. Students read their descriptions aloud in small groups, and try to guess what objects are described. This session is especially important if your students have not had lots of experience making careful and objective observations.

What You Need

For the teacher:
- ❏ a pencil, ruler, or other easily accessible object with which to model making good observations
- ❏ a pair of plastic-handled adult scissors or another object to serve as the mystery object you describe to the class (See "Getting Ready" for details.)

For each student:
- ❏ the Scientific Journal (masters at back of guide) or 1 copy of the Notes from an Extraterrestrial student sheet (master on page 25)
- ❏ a pencil
- ❏ *(optional)* file folders for Scientific Journal pages

Getting Ready

1. Select the mystery object that you plan to describe to your students. You can use the description of a pair of scissors that we have provided below or another object of your choosing. Have the object on hand to show students after they've had a chance to guess.

2. The Scientific Journal is simply a collection of all the student sheets needed for the entire unit. Decide if you want your students to record and save the work they do in this unit in the Scientific Journal (masters at back of guide) or whether you prefer that students use student sheets as needed. If you want to use the Scientific Journal we have provided, then duplicate one copy for each student, and choose the method below you prefer.

    a. Some teachers prefer to bind the pages together (staple them) and to pass the whole Scientific Journal out at the beginning of the unit.

b. Other teachers prefer to pass the pages of the Journal out session by session, in part to keep the suspense about later sessions, and in part to retain the flexibility of what becomes part of the Scientific Journal. In this case, pages can be punched (so students can add them to their three-ring binders), or contained in individual file folders.

Making Scientific Observations

1. Hold up an object, such as a pencil or a ruler, and ask your students to describe it **as if they are seeing it for the very first time.** Encourage them to make observations about the object, and for the time being not to use their prior knowledge or hearsay.

2. Emphasize that **observations are what you can detect using your senses.** Keep distinguishing between direct observations and other assumptions or inferences, or prior information and experience.

3. Provide a positive example of making observations without assumptions or inferences by describing an object (such as a pair of scissors) yourself in this manner. For example:

> This object appears to be made of some shiny metallic substance. It is about eight inches long and one end tapers to a point. The other end does not appear to be metallic, but some type of dull blue substance, which looks soft, but feels hard. This end has two openings, one of which is round, the other more like a flattened oval shape. When these openings are pulled apart, the tapered metallic end opens up into two prongs, both of which have a sharp edge and a dull edge. The sharp edges face each other.

4. After students have guessed what the object is, show it to them.

Introducing the Game:
Notes from an Extraterrestrial

1. Tell students they will be playing a game called Notes from an Extraterrestrial. Ask students to imagine that they are recent arrivals from another planet and are therefore seeing Earth-objects for the first time.

A number of GEMS guides assist students in making good observations and in comprehending the distinction between evidence and inference, or between observation and assumption. This distinction is central in Mystery Festival *and* Investigating Artifacts. *In* Oobleck: What Do Scientists Do? *students observe a substance, said to come from another planet, and carefully observe, discuss, and debate its properties. In* Animals in Action, *the class offers observations of animals in a classroom corral, such as "the animal is in the corner." At one point, the teacher deliberately inserts an assumption, such as "Look! The animal wants to get out." She then discusses this with the class, pointing out this is her own idea about why an animal is behaving a certain way—it is not a direct observation. Students replace this assumption with an observation, such as "the animal jumped up the wall."*

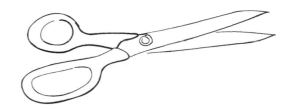

2. Tell them that in this game, each of them will get to secretly choose any object they want in the room. Their job will be to describe the object in writing, using only language an English-speaking extraterrestrial might use—excluding language that would identify the object. For example, in describing a plant, they could not use the word "leaves." Ask them to think of words they could use to describe leaves if they'd never seen them before.

3. When they are done writing their descriptions, they will read them aloud in a small group, and others will attempt to guess what they were describing.

4. Tell them that if they want to hold their object, they must get it surreptitiously and keep it hidden from their classmates. However, it may be better to just observe it from their seat.

This activity could be done indoors or outdoors.

In the commercially available game, "Taboo," participants are required to describe a given object without using certain "give-away" words.

Playing the Game

1. When students understand what they are to do, distribute the Scientific Journals (and ask students to turn to page 1) or Notes from an Extraterrestrial student sheets and let them begin. Circulate among the students, pointing out any "give-away" words you see and encouraging early finishers to add more description as necessary.

2. When most students are done writing their descriptions, get the attention of the class. Tell students they will work in groups of 4–6 to read the descriptions aloud, one-by-one. After each description is read, they can guess what they think it was. **No one is allowed to guess until they've heard the entire description of an object.**

3. If there is time, have students play the game a second time.

Conclusion

1. When the game is completed, get the attention of the class one more time. Tell them that the best scientists try to approach the world with fresh eyes, like an extraterrestrial might. Many important discoveries have been made when a scientist notices something that others overlooked, or challenges an unvalidated assumption that someone else made. For instance, Jupiter's moons weren't discovered until a man named Galileo noticed that some "stars" near

the planet Jupiter appeared to be moving. He then questioned whether they were actually stars. All the other scientists just assumed that those bright objects were stars. Their assumption contributed to preventing an important discovery from being made—until Galileo made his careful observations.

Moons of Jupiter is a GEMS unit that enables students to re-enact Galileo's discovery.

2. Tell the class that in this unit you would like them to continue to make careful and objective observations like they did today. The more details and the fewer assumptions they make, the better and more scientific their work will be.

3. Have students write the name of the object they observed on their student sheets, so you know what they were describing.

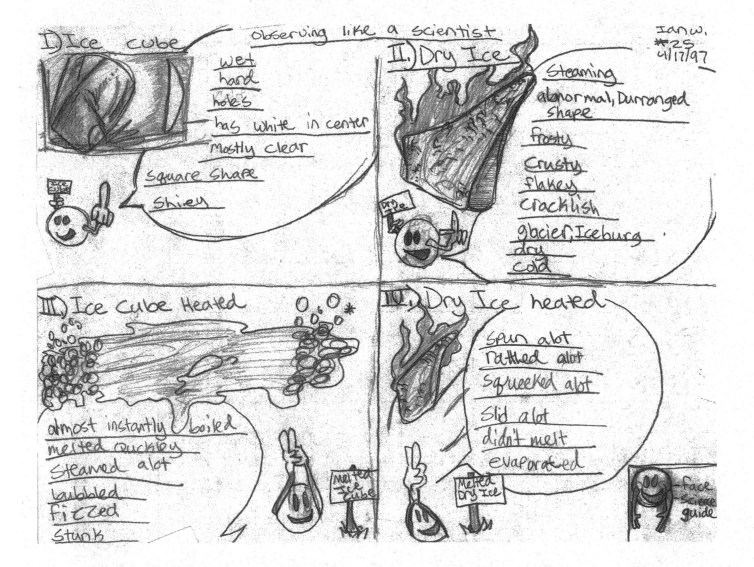

SCIENTIFIC JOURNAL

Name _____

© 1999 by The Regents of the University of California, LHS-GEMS. *Dry Ice Investigations*. May be duplicated for classroom use.

© 1999 by The Regents of the University of California, LHS-GEMS. *Dry Ice Investigations*. **May be duplicated for classroom use.**

Name _____

Notes from an Extraterrestrial

Object 1 _____

_____

_____

_____

_____

_____

_____

_____

Object 2 _____

_____

_____

_____

_____

_____

_____

_____

Session 2: Comparing Water Ice and Dry Ice

In this session students begin by making detailed observations of an ordinary ice cube—as if it were the first time they had ever seen one. They do the same with a piece of dry ice, while also making comparisons between the two substances. They then make observations and comparisons as the teacher adds energy (heat) to each piece of ice, first by placing an ice cube, then a piece of dry ice, on a hot plate (or electric skillet). Students are encouraged to come up with their own explanations for what they see happening in this demonstration.

The session ends with the introduction of a scientific motto, *Nullius in verba.* Loosely translated from the Latin, it means, "don't take anybody's word for it—see for yourself." This refers to a turning point in the history of science when the passing on of assumed ideas was replaced with emphasis on repeatability of results—results were considered valid when based on first-hand evidence that could be repeated with the same result by someone else.

What You Need

For the class:
- ❏ ice cubes (one ice cube per team of 4–6 students)
- ❏ dry ice (one approximately 1" piece per team of 4–6 students)
- ❏ small insulated container for storing pieces of dry ice
- ❏ hammer
- ❏ 2 cloths (old T-shirts or T-shirt sized rags)
- ❏ 1 or 2 pieces of butcher paper
- ❏ 1 marker
- ❏ masking tape

For the demonstration:
- ❏ 1 hot plate or electric skillet (See "Getting Ready" for details.)
- ❏ 1 extension cord (if needed for hot plate)
- ❏ 1 leather work glove (for the teacher to wear)
- ❏ *(optional)* 1 flat piece of metal to place on top of a burner or skillet with high sides (See "Getting Ready" for details.)

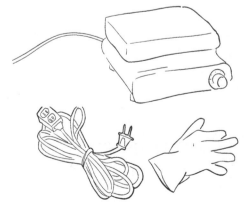

For each group of 4–6 students:
- ❏ 1 plastic cup with regular ice cube
- ❏ 1 plastic cup with dry ice

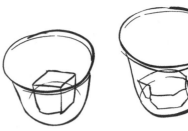

For each student:
- ❏ the Scientific Journal (masters at back of guide) or 1 copy each of the As if Seeing It for the First Time, Comparing Substances, and Adding Energy student sheets (masters on pages 34–36)
- ❏ a pencil

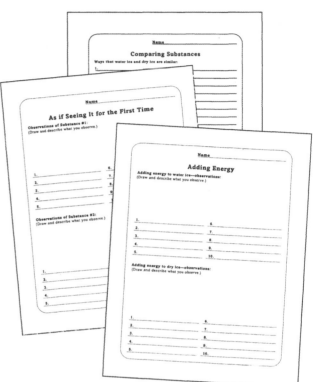

Getting Ready

Before the Day of the Activity

1. Plan how you will get dry ice. (See the section entitled "Obtaining and Maintaining Dry Ice" on page 7.) This session requires less than one slab for a class of 32 students.

2. Obtain a heat source for the teacher demonstration. In the demonstration you will need to quickly melt a water ice cube and sublime a piece of dry ice on a hot surface. A hot plate works best. You simply place the piece of ice directly on the preheated hot plate. A portable burner will work, but you will need to put a flat piece of metal on top of the burner to melt the ice on so students can see. An upside down stainless steel pie plate or a metal camping plate should work as a flat metal surface. An electric skillet can also be used, but if the skillet has tall sides that prevent students from viewing the ice melt, then you will also need a flat piece of metal to place across the top of the skillet, as mentioned above. Make sure that the skillet heats up the flat piece of metal by trying the demonstration ahead of time if possible. If the surface is not hot enough, the dry ice part of the demonstration will be less dramatic. Note: Teflon surfaces will not work.

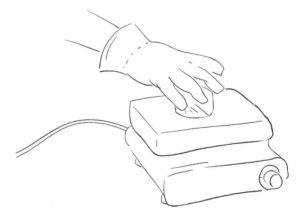

3. Acquire the remaining materials needed for this session.

4. Duplicate student sheets as necessary (masters on pages 34–36).

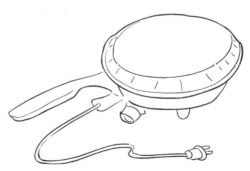

On the Day of the Activity

1. Have materials ready. During the activity you will be distributing, first a regular ice cube in a cup to each team of 4–6 students, and then a piece of dry ice in another cup to each team.

2. If you are using Scientific Journals, have them on hand or prepare to distribute the appropriate pages depending on how you are managing the journal.

Immediately Before Class

1. Lay a slab of dry ice on a towel, T-shirt, or other rag. Place another towel or cloth on top of it. Use the side of a hammer to break the dry ice through the rag. Break the dry ice into small pieces—approximately 1". Put one piece of dry ice in a cup for each team of 4–6 students. Stack the cups inside each other and place them in the small insulated container with any left over dry ice.

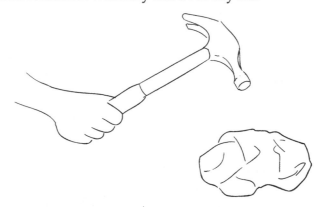

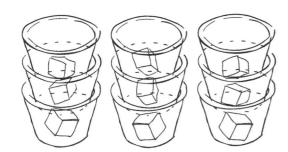

2. Put one water ice cube in a cup for each team of 4–6 students. Set these off to the side out of view from the students. Ideally these should be in a cooler so they won't melt. The cups can be stacked inside each other and placed in the same insulated container with the dry ice.

3. Plug the hot plate or skillet in a place where all students can see it but where they will not touch it accidentally. **This needs time to heat up so that it is nice and hot at the time of the teacher demonstration.** Set the leather glove next to the hot plate.

Observing Water Ice Cubes

1. Tell your students that today they are going to make observations about two objects, one of which they have seen many times before, and another that they may or may not have ever seen before. Let them know that their job is to **draw and write about everything** they are able to observe about each object. Tell them that for safety reasons, *they may not touch the objects with their skin or any part of their bodies.*

2. Distribute one clear plastic cup with an ice cube in it to each team of 4–6 students, and instruct them to begin drawing and describing their observations.

3. Have them record their observations on page 2 of their Scientific Journals if you are using them, or on the As if Seeing It for the First Time student sheets if you are not. **They should write down and keep track of all their observations and questions over the course of the unit.**

4. After a few minutes, with the whole class' attention, ask them to share a few of their observations. Once again, distinguish between descriptions that are and are not based on direct observation and assist students as needed in understanding this distinction.

Observing Dry Ice

1. Distribute another clear plastic cup with a small piece of dry ice in it to each team. Leave the cups of regular ice with students for now.

2. **Remind them that they may not touch the objects with their skin.** Tell them that they will have lots of opportunities to safely handle and experiment with this new substance later.

3. Tell your students to do the same things with the new object as they did with the first—carefully observe it and write down their observations with any drawings.

4. After a few minutes, regain the attention of the class, and ask them to share a few of their observations. Some students may mistakenly call it "hot ice." Many others are likely to know that the new substance they are observing is commonly called "dry ice." It is fine to begin referring to it by that name in class, but very important to emphasize to

One teacher we know has a gentle way of calling a student's attention to a statement that is more than a direct observation. If the student is using prior knowledge in her description, for example, "it's made of frozen water," he says, "you're being too smart."

the students that **just knowing a name doesn't explain how a substance behaves or what it really is.**

5. Some students may also start talking about carbon dioxide. Once again, stress that there'll be more information later on, but for now the main idea is to observe the behavior of this substance **as if for the first time.** This means consciously not taking into account our own prior knowledge or any other assumptions not based on direct sensory experience—what you see is what you get!

Comparing and Contrasting

1. Now ask students to continue their observations, focusing this time on what they can directly observe about the similarities and differences between the two substances.

2. Have them write down these comparing observations on page 3 of their journal, or on the Comparing Substances student sheet.

3. After a few minutes, ask one member of each group to bring both of their cups to a location you specify where they will not be a distraction.

4. Regain the attention of the whole class, and ask them to briefly share some of their comparisons.

5. Encourage students to write down any questions they may have.

Adding Heat

1. Gather the class so they can all see the hot plate/skillet teacher demonstration. You may need to have groups change places to allow for better viewing.

2. Tell the class you're going to place a water ice cube on the hot plate/skillet. Ask them what they think will happen. Ask them to observe carefully, once again as if for the first time. Use a leather glove to handle and control the ice cube, while taking care not to touch the hot element. As the ice sizzles, steams, and evaporates, elicit more observations. Later, have your students record them on page 4 of their journal, or on the Adding Energy student sheet.

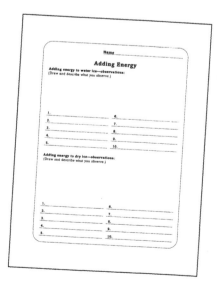

3. Encourage them to come up with their own explanations about what they just observed, as if they had never seen it before. Ask them where the ice appeared to "go." Some may say it looked like it went into the air, while others may say that it appeared to sink into the hot plate.

4. Next, tell students you are going to do the same with a piece of dry ice. Ask for their predictions about what they think will happen. While still wearing the leather glove, place a piece of dry ice on the hot plate. The dry ice will tend to slide around, so you will need to actively keep it on the hot plate. You can make it spin and vibrate, even squeak, by turning it and by pushing down on it against the metal surface.

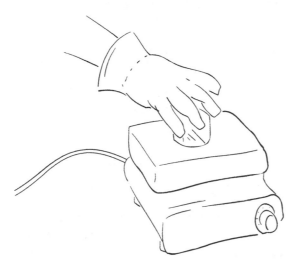

5. Again elicit observations and comparisons from your students. Tell them to record these observations, and encourage them to try to explain what they just saw as if it were for the first time (for many students it probably will be). **Be sure to keep students from touching the hot plate/ skillet while it is hot.**

Important Note: Some students may discuss "melting" for both substances. At this point, simply accept all their observations and comments. **Melting** is when a solid changes into a liquid when heat is added, as the water ice does. Dry ice **sublimes**—it does not melt. Sublimation is when a solid, like dry ice, changes directly into a gas when heat is added, without first changing into a liquid state. (Technically, sublimation also includes the process of cooling the same substance until it turns back into a solid.) **Be careful not to introduce this concept and term too early in this unit. It is introduced directly much later on, after students have much more experience with the substance and its behavior. Be sure to allow your stu-**

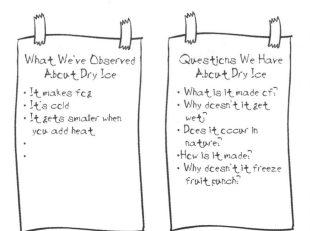

What We've Observed About Dry Ice

- It makes fog
- It's cold
- It gets smaller when you add heat
-
-

Questions We Have About Dry Ice

- What is it made of?
- Why doesn't it get wet?
- Does it occur in nature?
- How is it made?
- Why doesn't it freeze fruit punch?

One teacher tells her students that she likes working with middle school students most of all. She believes that it is the time of life when open thinking is most likely to happen, in part because middle schoolers are capable of complex thought and yet their minds are not yet overly biased with lots of assumptions and previous knowledge.

Nullius in verba

dents the opportunity to discover, wonder about, try to explain, and debate the way that dry ice changes directly from solid to gas before giving them scientific terms for what happens.

6. Begin a class list on the butcher paper to help summarize and keep track of what the class is observing and of questions students have: "What We've Observed About Dry Ice," and "Questions We Have About Dry Ice." With students referring to their written notes, facilitate a brief class discussion to start off the lists in both categories. You can add to these lists in subsequent sessions. **Note:** In Activity 4, students will be referring to the class list of "Questions We Have About Dry Ice" so it is especially important to keep this list current.

Thinking Like a Scientist

1. Again, point out to your students that they are now thinking in the same way that scientists do—the ability to carefully observe and to see things **as if for the first time** has led to many breakthroughs in understanding. Many great scientists, like Galileo, have dared to question the scientific facts of their time. Some people may even have thought these scientists were crazy, but they turned out to be brilliant "Michael Jordans of the mind" who were ahead of their time and moved science forward because they dared to question.

2. Write *"Nullius in verba"* on the board. Explain that this is the motto of London's Royal Society, a group of scientists that began in 1662. Freely translated from Latin, it means, "take nobody's word for it; see for yourself." Observing things for themselves—like your students just did and will do lots more of—fits this idea. Let students know that the motto also is a way of saying that doing science involves gathering first-hand evidence through experiments that can be repeated by others. This connects to a key idea in modern science—that if only one person gets a result from an experiment and it can't be duplicated by others, then the result is not accepted by the scientific community.

Point out that life is too short to allow every person to "find out (everything!) for themselves." In fact, even while London's Royal Society of scientists took on the motto, *Nullius in verba,* they also built their work upon the work of others. Once something was verified by several different scientists, they acknowledged that as a "truth" accepted by the community of scientists—until it became "disproved" or modified by others. A good scientist keeps a fresh open mind about what s/he sees but also relies on the verified work of other scientists.

3. Explain that they are going to have a chance to think up and perform their own investigations with dry ice later in the unit. Although some of them may already know some things about dry ice, they should still think and act as if they have never heard anything about it before—they should take nobody else's word for it—so they can **find out for themselves.** This fresh eye might enable them to make new discoveries about dry ice!

4. At the end of the session, draw your students' attention to the cups of water ice and of dry ice to observe how they have changed.

One teacher flashed Nullius in verba on an electronic sign for two weeks with no explanation. He had his students and their parents digging to guess the significance. Another teacher posted a sign saying, Nullius in verba outside the classroom and had other students in the school wondering what it meant. It became the secret motto of her students.

In 1999, Dr. Ian Carmichael, renowned geologist and Director of Lawrence Hall of Science, was inducted into the Royal Society of London. He traveled to London and signed the book that all past members have signed. His name appears with names such as Isaac Newton, John Dalton, and Charles Darwin! Over 300 years after its inception, the Royal Society of London continues on, as an organization recognizing many of the "best" inquirers into the natural world.

Caitlin
4/18/97

Lesson I

Investigation

I put a small piece of dry ice in a vile about three inches tall. Then I filled the vile a little less than half way with water I stretched a baloon over the top.

cold water
dry ice

The vile got foggy as the balloon was filling up with fog. First the balloon looked like a little ball hanging over the side of the vile. Then after about ten seconds it began to stand straight up.

Explanation

I think dry ice is water and air crammed into one. When water is put on it, the dry ice is being converted. The water is forcing the air out. So when the air was being pushed out of the vile it was being blown into the balloon. This was what I think was happening. I think. Sort of. Maybe.

© 1999 by The Regents of the University of California, LHS-GEMS. *Dry Ice Investigations.* **May be duplicated for classroom use.**

Name _____

As if Seeing It for the First Time

Observations of Substance #1:
(Draw and describe what you observe.)

1. _____
2. _____
3. _____
4. _____
5. _____

6. _____
7. _____
8. _____
9. _____
10. _____

Observations of Substance #2:
(Draw and describe what you observe.)

1. _____
2. _____
3. _____
4. _____
5. _____

6. _____
7. _____
8. _____
9. _____
10. _____

Name _____

Comparing Substances

Ways that water ice and dry ice are similar:

1. _____

2. _____

3. _____

4. _____

5. _____

6. _____

7. _____

8. _____

9. _____

10. _____

Ways that water ice and dry ice are different:

1. _____

2. _____

3. _____

4. _____

5. _____

6. _____

7. _____

8. _____

9. _____

10. _____

© 1999 by The Regents of the University of California, LHS-GEMS. *Dry Ice Investigations*. **May be duplicated for classroom use.**

© 1999 by The Regents of the University of California, LHS-GEMS. *Dry Ice Investigations*. **May be duplicated for classroom use.**

Name _____

Adding Energy

Adding energy to water ice—observations:
(Draw and describe what you observe.)

1. _____   6. _____

2. _____   7. _____

3. _____   8. _____

4. _____   9. _____

5. _____   10. _____

Adding energy to dry ice—observations:
(Draw and describe what you observe.)

1. _____   6. _____

2. _____   7. _____

3. _____   8. _____

4. _____   9. _____

5. _____   10. _____

Session 3: Matter and Energy

In this session, students are presented with a particulate model of matter, something that took scientists centuries to develop and verify, as it involves things that are impossible to observe directly. Students apply this model to their understanding of the demonstration in the last session, when water and dry ice were placed on a hot plate. They work in small groups to discuss four different, but common conceptions for what happens to ice at the molecular level when energy (heat) is added.

After debating these different ideas, students learn what many scientists and much scientific work have confirmed—when heated, the molecules in ice stay the same size and the same shape, they just move faster and farther apart. The session ends with the teacher sharing some information about the actual temperature of the two different kinds of ice and some related safety tips about dry ice.

The goal of this session is to have students first share their ideas about the particulate nature of matter and then, through interaction and discussion, modify their ideas to become more correct. This process parallels what the scientific community does. Students (and adults!) hold many common misconceptions about this topic (see the "Behind the Scenes" section on page 133 for more information about these misconceptions). **Research indicates that the best way to get people to correct their misconceptions is to provide them with revealing experiences and allow time for them to compare and discuss alternative ideas/explanations so they themselves discover the flaws in their own thinking.** The purpose of the Energy and Matter Questionnaire is to spur that critical discussion of alternative ideas.

Classes who are not used to sustaining small group discussions may be challenged by the format of this activity. The value of students arguing different viewpoints is tremendous and worth the effort to cultivate (in both this and other units). Some teachers whose students were not ready for small group discussions chose to have students hold discussions in pairs, and others used a large group format. You may want to modify the format appropriately for the abilities and experience of your class.

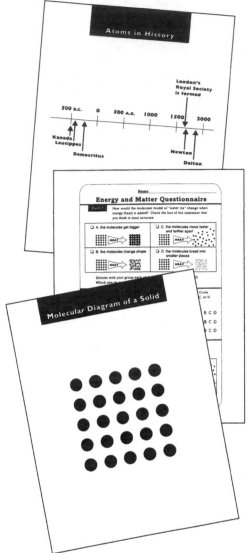

What You Need

For the class:
- ❏ an overhead transparency each of the Atoms in History (master on page 45), Molecular Diagram of a Solid (master on page 46), and the Energy and Matter Questionnaire (master on page 47)
- ❏ 3 plastic Petri dishes (about 4" in diameter) with top and bottom. (Alternatively, 6 clear deli container lids can be used; 3 as tops and 3 as bottoms.)
- ❏ a handful of BBs
- ❏ glue or tape
- ❏ 1 marker
- ❏ overhead projector
- ❏ extension cord (if needed for overhead projector)

For each student:
- ❏ the Scientific Journal (masters at back of guide) or 1 copy of the Energy and Matter Questionnaire student sheet (master on page 47)
- ❏ a pencil

Getting Ready

Before the Day of the Activity

1. Make BB models—one each to represent a solid, a liquid, and a gas. To one Petri dish add several BBs, to another add fewer BBs, and to the third add even fewer. Glue or tape the tops of the Petri dishes to the bottoms of the dishes so the BBs will not fly out when the dishes are shaken. Label or write "solid" on the side of the dish with the most BBs; "gas" on the side of the dish with the fewest BBs; and "liquid" on the side of the third dish. These models will be used more than once in this unit.

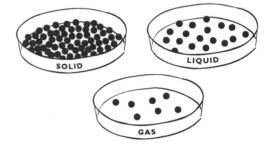

2. Make an overhead transparency each of the Atoms in History (master on page 45), Molecular Diagram of a Solid (master on page 46), and the Energy and Matter Question-naire (master on page 47).

3. Duplicate student sheets as necessary (master on page 47).

On the Day of the Activity

1. Set up the overhead projector and place the overhead transparencies and the BB models near by.

2. If you are using Scientific Journals, have them on hand or prepare to distribute the appropriate pages depending on how you are managing the journal.

GO! Introduce a Particulate Model

1. Tell students that about 150 years after London's Royal Society adopted the motto *Nullius in verba*, a scientist named John Dalton, also a member of London's Royal Society, suggested a "wild" explanation for the many observations he had made about the world. **He proposed the idea that all matter is composed of tiny, moving particles called *atoms*.** Write this on the board.

If your students have not previously been introduced to the word "mat-ter," take the opportunity to do so now. Tell them that matter is the word we use to describe all of the "stuff" in the universe. Anything that has weight (mass) and takes up space is matter.

Let students know that John Dalton was not the first to propose this explanation. Turn on the overhead projector and show the Atoms in History overhead.

- Dozens of centuries before Dalton, Kanada, a Hindu from India, wrote about "small eternal particles in perpetual motion." He was the first to suggest the name "atom."

The atomic theory occurs in the Vaisesika system, and is attributed to Kanada (500 BC?) and further developed in later Buddhist and Jainist works from the second century BC. The atom is first called "anu," meaning small, and later "paramanu," meaning absolutely small. It is described as indestructible, spherical, and six times smaller than the smallest mote in a sunbeam. In these works from ancient India, atoms are thought to possess color, taste, and smell and to associate first in pairs, and then in larger groupings of pairs. (See A Short History of Chemistry *by J.R. Partington, Dover, New York, 1989.)*

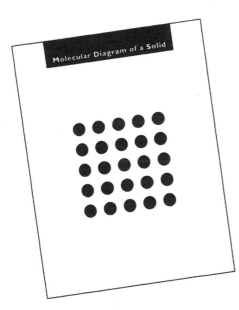

- In about 500 B.C., a Greek philosopher, Leucippus, spoke of "tiny particles of various kinds separated by space through which they travel."

- Close to the same time another Greek, Democritus, "the laughing philosopher" believed that matter is composed of "empty space and an infinite number of invisible atoms, i.e. small particles."

- In the 17th century, Newton suggested that "God in the beginning formed matter in solid, massy, hard, impenetrable, movable particles."

Tell students that while Dalton was not the first to suggest the explanation (or model) of moving atoms, he—and all the others before him—were considered to have weird ideas by many people. While Dalton could not prove that his atomic theory was correct at the time, he used his idea that matter is made of **moving, spherical atoms** to explain and figure out many more things. It would take another 150 years to prove that this theory of matter was largely correct. Resist the temptation to get bogged down in a discussion about molecular theory now. This will happen later in the session.

2. Show the Molecular Diagram of a Solid transparency. Say that this diagram gives a general idea of what scientists think a solid (like ice or dry ice) might look like, if we could see the individual particles.

3. Explain that we now know more than Dalton did, but there is still much we don't know. Things we **do** know include:

- All matter is made of atoms, which are far too small to see directly through an ordinary microscope.

- Individual atoms combine to form molecules. (Dalton actually suggested this, too.) That is what these dots represent.

- There is space between molecules. (Point out the space between in the model.)

- Molecules are always moving.

4. Tell students that this diagram is a **model** that can help us think about and understand something that can't be seen—in the case of molecules because they are so infinitesimally small.

5. Point out that this model is good at showing the physical arrangement of molecules, but it is limited in that it does not show the movement of molecules. Show students the more dynamic BB model of a solid. Place the BB model on the overhead projector and lightly jiggle the BBs back and forth so they appear to vibrate. Continue moving the BBs, and again point out that molecules in matter are always moving. Point out the space between the molecules. Turn off the overhead projector.

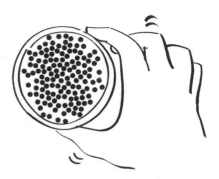

6. Tell the class that water ice (and water) is made of two hydrogen (H) atoms and one oxygen (O) atom. That is why water is called H_2O. Write H_2O on the board. A molecule of carbon dioxide is made of one carbon (C) atom and two oxygen (O) atoms. That is why carbon dioxide is called CO_2. Write CO_2 on the board. Point out that water and ice and dry ice would look similar if we could see them at a molecular level; the main difference is the shape of the individual molecules. There is still space between them, and they are still always moving.

What Happens When You Add Energy?

Part 1

1. Ask students to think about the demonstration you presented last session when you put ice on the hot plate. You were adding energy to the ice—heat energy. Ask students to recall what happened when energy was added to water ice; to dry ice.

2. Turn on the overhead projector. Show the Energy and Matter Questionnaire. Tell the class that you are going to challenge them to figure out how the molecular model of water ice might change when energy is added. Let students know they'll be working in groups using this questionnaire.

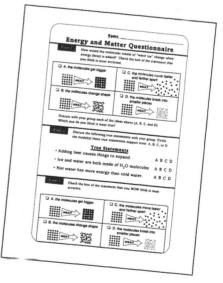

3. Tell students that when they're in their groups they should first read Part 1 of the questionnaire by themselves and then check the box of the idea that makes the most sense to them. Emphasize that they should not worry if their idea is right or wrong or the same or different from someone else's. They'll get to change their ideas if they want in Part 3. Then students should discuss their ideas in their small group.

4. Distribute the Energy and Matter Questionnaire or instruct students to turn to page 5 in their Scientific Journal. Put the students together in groups of 4–6.

5. Have individual students begin with Part 1. Circulate among the groups encouraging discussion.

6. After 5–10 minutes, gain the attention of the whole class. Remind them that the thinking and discussing they are doing now, as they try to explain how matter behaves, is something that scientists do all the time. This is what John Dalton did with other chemists in his day. Point out that changing one's mind can be the sign of a great and open thinker!

7. Ask for a few volunteers to share their thinking about models A, B, C, or D and the reasoning behind their thinking. Spend just long enough to get the discussion going in the large group. You will be having this discussion again later in the session, so you don't want the students to get "talked out."

Part 2

1. Explain that scientists typically take into account information that other scientists have determined to be true as they discuss possible models. This can help clarify or disprove a model. Tell them that that is what they will do right now in Part 2 of the questionnaire. Point out that Part 2 lists three "true statements" that represent things that many different scientists have determined to be true. Ask them to discuss the statements, one by one, and circle the letter of the model that these true statements best support.

2. Have the groups begin with Part 2.

3. Circulate among groups reminding them to consider the three bulleted true statements as they talk about the various ideas.

Part 3

1. After about 5–10 minutes (depending on how engaged your students are) tell students that you would like them, in the next couple of minutes, to go on to Part 3 of the questionnaire. It's fine to talk with others in the group about the idea they choose; they should each check the box of the idea that now makes the most sense to *them*. Tell them not to change what they wrote in Part 1, even if they have now changed their minds.

What Scientists Have Found Out

1. When students have completed Part 3 of the questionnaire, gain the attention of the whole class. Again mention that this kind of thinking and discussion is something that scientists do all the time, and that a trait of a great thinker is someone who can change his or her mind when confronted with new evidence or information. Ask for a few volunteers to again share their thinking about models A, B, C, or D and why they think what they do.

2. Do your best to elicit problems with models A, B, C, and D. Research shows that students will not abandon a current understanding until they see a problem with it. Some of this will have happened in the small group discussions; some will come from students in the big group discussion.

3. After several students have shared their ideas and some discussion has occurred, tell the class that over time, with many scientists repeating and confirming each other's results, it has been determined that model C is most accurate. Reiterate that when you add heat (energy), molecules move faster and farther apart. They are still the same molecules but they have more energy and take up more space.

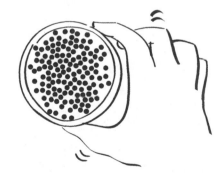

4. Use all three BB models to model what happens when energy is added to matter. Do this by beginning with the "solid" model, moving the Petri dish back and forth slowly so the BBs vibrate. Then say that you are adding energy. Quickly replace the "solid" model with the "liquid" model and move the dish of BBs faster so the BBs appear to move "fluidly." Point out that the molecules are moving faster and farther apart. Then say that you will add more energy. Quickly replace the "liquid" model with the "gas" model and move the dish of BBs back and forth rapidly, so the BBs appear as a blur. Point out that the more energy you add, the more energy (movement) the molecules have. **The point you want to illustrate here, is that with increased energy, molecules move faster and farther apart.**

Note: Avoid introducing the concepts of phases and phase change now, unless it comes up from the students. The BB models will be used again to focus on how these changes correspond with changes in the phase of a substance.

Temperature and Safety

1. End the session by saying that in the next session, they will be working more with dry ice. For them to do that safely, you need to tell them a little bit about how cold dry ice really is!

2. Draw a thermometer on your chalkboard, and make a mark to show where 32°F above zero is (or 0°C). Tell your students that 32°F above zero (or 0°C) is very cold, the temperature of water ice cubes.

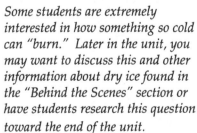

    a. Make a mark at 0°F (or 18°C below zero). Ask them to imagine how cold that is.

    b. Make a mark at 50°F below zero (or 46°C below zero), and then tell them that although this is very cold, it is still not as cold as dry ice.

    c. Make a mark at 110°F below zero (or 79°C below zero), and tell them that's how cold dry ice is. Warn them that dry ice is cold enough to "burn" their skin if touched for any length of time, and caution them again that they are **not to touch it with their skin.**

3. Let your students know that dry ice is a potentially harmful substance, and that—**if anyone acts in an unsafe way with it, they will need to sit out the rest of the class session, away from the materials.**

Some students are extremely interested in how something so cold can "burn." Later in the unit, you may want to discuss this and other information about dry ice found in the "Behind the Scenes" section or have students research this question toward the end of the unit.

Atoms in History

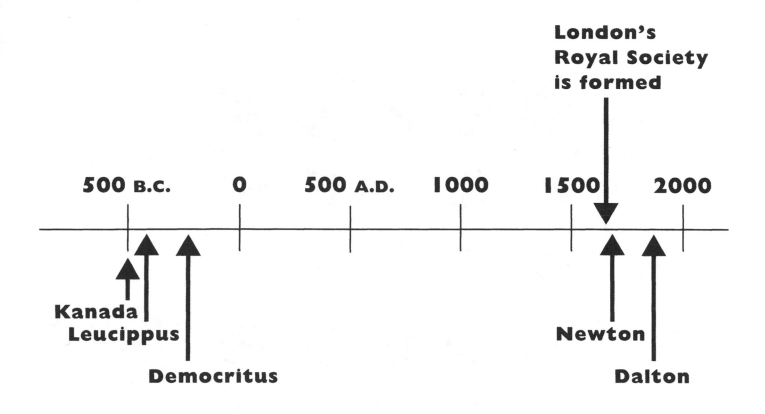

London's Royal Society is formed

500 B.C. 0 500 A.D. 1000 1500 2000

Kanada
Leucippus

Democritus

Newton

Dalton

© 1999 by The Regents of the University of California, LHS-GEMS. *Dry Ice Investigations*. **May be duplicated for classroom use.**

© 1999 by The Regents of the University of California, LHS-GEMS. *Dry Ice Investigations.* **May be duplicated for classroom use.**

Name _____

Energy and Matter Questionnaire

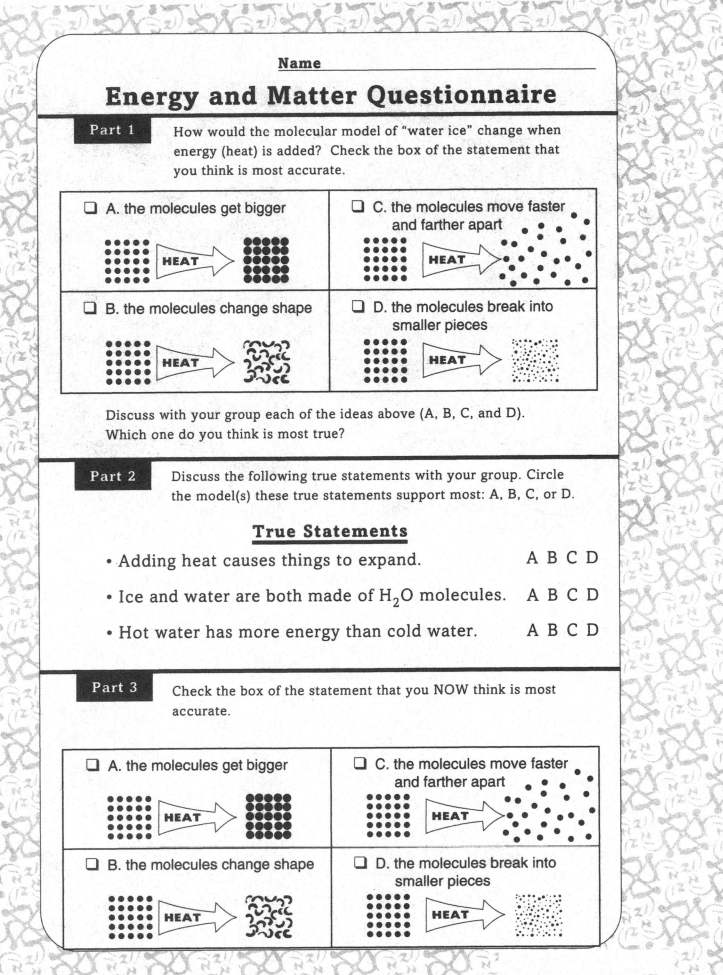

Part 1 How would the molecular model of "water ice" change when energy (heat) is added? Check the box of the statement that you think is most accurate.

☐ A. the molecules get bigger

HEAT

☐ C. the molecules move faster and farther apart

HEAT

☐ B. the molecules change shape

HEAT

☐ D. the molecules break into smaller pieces

HEAT

Discuss with your group each of the ideas above (A, B, C, and D). Which one do you think is most true?

Part 2 Discuss the following true statements with your group. Circle the model(s) these true statements support most: A, B, C, or D.

True Statements

• Adding heat causes things to expand.   A B C D

• Ice and water are both made of H_2O molecules.   A B C D

• Hot water has more energy than cold water.   A B C D

Part 3 Check the box of the statement that you NOW think is most accurate.

☐ A. the molecules get bigger

HEAT

☐ C. the molecules move faster and farther apart

HEAT

☐ B. the molecules change shape

HEAT

☐ D. the molecules break into smaller pieces

HEAT

© 1999 by The Regents of the University of California, LHS-GEMS. Dry Ice Investigations. May be duplicated for classroom use.

Activity 2:
Systematic Observation

Overview

In this three-session activity, students are guided through the processes of exploration and systematic observation as ways of finding out more about the world.

In Session 1, they are given a collection of materials with which to explore dry ice in an open-ended way. Throughout this exploration, the teacher sets the scene for wondering why, continuing the theme of practicing key scientific habits of mind.

In Session 2, students are guided through a more systematic observation of a phenomenon, as they investigate what happens when you put dry ice in soap solution. This experience leads them to discover that dry ice changes from a solid to a gas, something that some students have not yet figured out. At the end of the session, they are introduced to the language and system of phases and phase change, and again revisit a molecular model for explaining these changes.

In Session 3, students attempt to solve the mystery of the floating bubbles as they use their new-found knowledge about dry ice to explain why soap bubbles float in a container of dry ice.

The objectives of this activity are to: provide opportunity for free exploration and systematic observation; experience the relative power of different ways of finding out; provide students with practice in wondering why; encourage students to take the risk of creatively thinking of and suggesting an explanation; increase the care and rigor with which explanations are made; allow students to discover that dry ice changes from a solid to a gas; introduce the language of phase changes including sublimation; and introduce phase change on a molecular level.

Session 1: Exploring Dry Ice

In this session, groups of students are given the exciting opportunity to freely explore dry ice. With common materials and simple equipment to assist them in their explorations, students are challenged to make discoveries, question, and think for themselves. While strong emphasis continues on the scientific need for careful and detailed **observation**, this session introduces a new emphasis—coming up with possible **explanations**. Students are asked to verbally come up with their own explanations to try to explain what they observe—with the understanding that during this class, no explanation is "too stupid" to share. For homework, students write about these initial explanations.

Some classes (or individual students) have difficulty gaining the initial confidence to venture possible explanations. That is why all explanations, no matter how unrealistic, are encouraged. It is important to communicate that all explanations should be subject to constant revision, as we learn more. Just as we saw in the case of early great scientists, what we first think can almost always be refined to be more true. Later in the unit, as students gain more familiarity with the behavior of dry ice their explanations will become more refined.

You'll find your students to be enthusiastic, inventive, and ingenious—making use of many materials available in the classroom and coming up with many questions they may want to pursue more fully later in the unit. Be sure to re-emphasize safety precautions as needed and to maintain a sense of continual questioning and further exploration throughout.

Note: We strongly recommend that soap or bubble solution (or the liquid soap in dispensers found in some classrooms) **NOT** be used in these initial experiments. Ideally, eliminate any possibility of its use in this session. If your students have access to soap powder to make soap solution, tell them not to use it at this time—everyone will get a chance to use it in explorations in the very next session!

This session is intended to encourage free student exploration. Some teachers, however, especially those with younger students or those whose students have less experience working in teams, have decided to add some structure by picking one of the tests on the Dry Ice Challenges student sheet and working through that test as a class, in teams, before letting the teams explore on their own. In our experience, however, most students quickly catch on and come up with their own ideas.

What You Need

For the class:
- ❏ dry ice (about 1 slab)
- ❏ hammer
- ❏ 2 cloths (old T-shirts or T-shirt sized rags)
- ❏ small insulated container for storing pieces of dry ice
- ❏ 1 box of ziplock sandwich bags
- ❏ 1 box of drinking straws
- ❏ 1 cold water dispenser, such as a dishtub or cooler (sending kids to the sink can work too, if you have water in your classroom)
- ❏ 1 hot water dispenser (such as an electric coffee maker)

For each group of 4–6 students:
- ❏ 1 tray
- ❏ 2 tweezers
- ❏ 2 balloons (9" or 12" balloons both work well)
- ❏ 2 clear plastic cups
- ❏ 1 or 2 cups that will not melt with hot water in them (such as heavy plastic or styrofoam)
- ❏ 2 medicine droppers
- ❏ 2 plastic spoons (or 4–6 leather gloves)
- ❏ 2 small plastic flasks or vials (without lids)
- ❏ 2 pennies or other metal objects
- ❏ 1 ziplock sandwich bag
- ❏ (optional) 2–3 one-third pages of the Dry Ice Challenges (master on page 62)

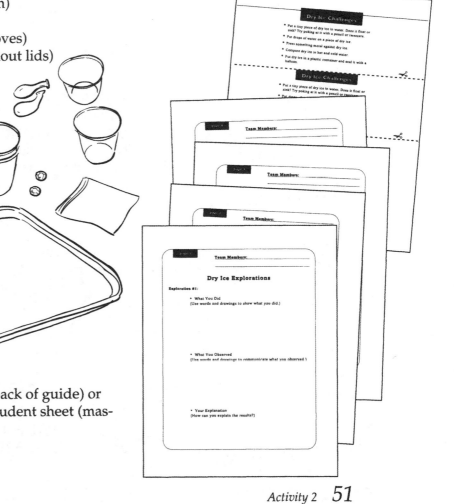

For each student:
- ❏ the Scientific Journal (masters at back of guide) or the 4-page Dry Ice Explorations student sheet (master on pages 58–61)
- ❏ a pencil

Getting Ready

Before the Day of the Activity

1. Plan how you will get dry ice. (See the section entitled "Obtaining and Maintaining Dry Ice" on page 7.) This session requires about one slab of dry ice for a class of 32 students.

2. Obtain hot and cold water dispensers. Students will need a way to access hot and cold water for their explorations with dry ice. The water need not be very hot or very cold, but different enough in temperature so that students can test the effect of this variable. An electric coffee pot or an "air pot" work particularly well as hot water dispensers because of the easy and safe way students can dispense the water (with a spigot or by pressing a button). Other large insulated thermos-type containers can work well too.

3. Acquire the remaining materials needed for this session.

4. Duplicate student sheets as necessary (masters on pages 58–62). If you have decided to use them, copy the Dry Ice Challenges student sheets and cut them into thirds.

On the Day of the Activity

1. Set up one tray for each group of 4–6 students containing: 2 plastic cups, 2 tweezers, 2 balloons, 1 or 2 cups that can hold hot water, 2 medicine droppers, 2 plastic spoons (or 4–6 leather gloves), 2 small plastic flasks/vials (without lids), 2 pennies or other metal objects, and a ziplock bag.

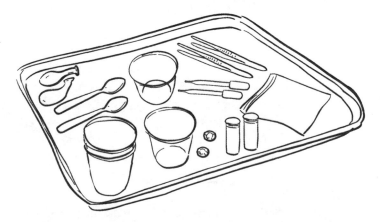

2. If you are using Scientific Journals, have them on hand or prepare to distribute the appropriate pages depending on how you are managing the journal.

3. In a central location, place the following materials: trays of equipment, drinking straws, hot water dispenser, cold water dispenser, and dry ice in an insulated container (see below).

Immediately Before Class

1. Fill and plug in the hot water heater (or heat water to fill your insulated hot water dispenser).

2. Lay a slab of dry ice on a towel, T-shirt, or other rag. Place another towel or cloth on top of it. Use the side of a hammer to break the dry ice through the rag. Break the dry ice into small pieces, and put them in a small insulated container.

GO !

Seeking Explanations

1. Explain that in this session they will get to make their own discoveries about dry ice. Re-emphasize safety rules and concerns. Explain that they will again be working in teams of 4–6 students.

2. Tell your students that when they make an interesting discovery their initial reaction might be to say something along the lines of, "whoa, coooool!" Scientists might also react the same way—and then they would take it to the next step.

3. The next step is to come up with some kind of **explanation** of what they are observing. Remind them that in this class, no observation is too simple or basic to say out loud, and no explanation is "too stupid." They should think creatively and even come up with what they think might be "wild" explanations. They should stretch their mental muscles! Like all good scientists, they will get a chance to revise their explanations to be more correct as they learn more.

4. Emphasize that they need to take the time, like scientists do, to write down their observations and to discuss explanations together.

You may want to make a Dry Ice Safety chart, as a reminder of safety rules and precautions.

If students do not push themselves to come up with explanations, you may need to stop their explorations very briefly, to remind them to discuss explanations for what they have observed up to that point before continuing. This will also help those students who may be feeling intimidated by the idea of "explanations."

Introducing the Materials

1. Briefly show your students the materials they will have available to them during their investigations:

Dry ice. Tell your students that there is a limited supply of dry ice available—they need to use it sparingly. Explain that it's much more interesting to use small amounts of dry ice in a variety of different experiments than to dump it all into one large experiment. Instruct them not to waste their portion by simply dumping more dry ice into an experiment just to make it bigger.

Tweezers/spoons/gloves. Let students know that they can touch the other materials with their bare hands, but not the dry ice. Point out that tweezers and spoons are very effective tools for safe handling of dry ice. If you are supplying gloves, tell your students that using **dry** leather gloves is a safe way of handling dry ice (wet leather gloves don't work). Tell them that in order to keep the leather gloves dry and effective they should not touch wet things with them. Also let them know that they'll use just one glove from a pair.

Water. Show your students where they can get cold and hot water. Show them how to safely dispense the hot water. Warn them not to touch the hot water or the sides of the coffee pot if you are using one. Demonstrate how they are to carry the cups of hot water with **two hands** back to their tables, as a reminder to themselves that they are carrying something very hot.

Cups. Show your students which cups they may and may not use for hot water.

Flasks/vials, balloons, and ziplock bags. Warn your students that **they are not to put dry ice in airtight containers. The only exceptions are: ziplock bags, or a container sealed with a balloon** (such as a plastic vial with a balloon over its mouth). **Also warn them that they are not to use glass containers with dry ice.**

Straws. Show your students where the straws are kept if they decide to use any. Warn them that they are not to use them to inhale dry ice gas, since it is unsafe.

*Be sure **not** to model unsafe behaviors with dry ice yourself, such as tossing it back and forth in your bare hands, or putting it in your mouth. These are not only examples of bad role-modeling for young people, they can also result in injury.*

If you are using styrofoam cups, you may wish to point out that it is a non-recyclable material. Encourage your students to allow for their reuse by not poking holes in them.

Warning: *If dry ice is placed in an airtight container, pressure from the gas released from the dry ice may burst the container.*

Scientific Journals/or student sheets. Again, remind your students that they are to record what they do and their observations of what happens. Tell them that while they are exploring, they can record in a more sketchy, less complete way. For homework they'll be using these notes to do a more careful job.

Starting the Dry Ice Explorations

1. Ask a volunteer from each team to get a tray of equipment for their team.

2. Distribute the Dry Ice Explorations student sheets or instruct students to turn to pages 6A–6D in their journal. If you're using them, have the Dry Ice Challenges student sheets ready for distribution later in the session.

3. Distribute a small amount of dry ice to each group (about 1 or 2 tablespoons). Periodically distribute more as needed throughout the class period, giving each table approximately the same amounts to be fair. **The less you give them at first, the better they are about making more detailed observations and not wasting it.** You may wish to give each team a slightly larger amount each time you make your dry ice distribution rounds.

4. Circulate to assist students as needed. Meander, **ask questions,** lend a hand, make suggestions, encourage them to record observations, and enforce safety rules.

5. It is very important that you visit every team, and at least help them get started with their explanations by asking them questions about their explorations, and by responding to their explanations in an encouraging manner. Don't accept "I don't know."

6. Here are some sample "starter" questions:

- Where is the stuff that is filling up the balloon/bag coming from?

- How could so much gas/air be coming from such a tiny piece of dry ice?

- If the container is closed, and more "stuff" can't get in, why are the contents taking up more space and filling the balloon?

One teacher doled out small amounts of dry ice during her first four periods of the day. She allowed the students in her last period to use the remaining dry ice in larger amounts and noticed that their explorations were much less carefully done. Less is more!

- Why do you think the water rolls off the dry ice?

- Why do tiny floating pieces of dry ice move away from other objects?

7. If you notice that many students in your class are not proposing explanations and discussing the "why" of the phenomena they observe, consider stopping the class explorations very briefly, and telling them to do nothing but share explanations for a minute or two. Then allow them to resume their explorations, but remind them to keep coming up with explanations, so the explorations won't have to be stopped again.

Important Note: With the emphasis on explaining the phenomena students are seeing, many teachers have wanted to know the "correct" explanations themselves. We have included lots of information about dry ice and the phenomena that your students might observe in the "Behind the Scenes" section beginning on page 133. However, we caution you from immediately supplying students with "right answers" or of even emphasizing correctness at this point in the unit. During this session, the goal is for your students to take the risk of suggesting an explanation and of modeling the important habit of revising explanations. Some of the phenomena they will be seeing are fairly complicated to explain in a complete and correct way. Thus the emphasis, rather than being on the "correct" explanation, should be on the process of coming up with their best explanations. By asking challenging questions, you can help students logically construct stronger and stronger explanations. During later sessions, students will be challenged to try and explain some phenomena whose "correct" explanations are more within their grasp, and to construct investigations to test the veracity of their explanations.

8. After *at least* 10 minutes of free exploration, you may wish to give each pair of students the Dry Ice Challenges sheet. This allows the students to discover some aspects of dry ice which they might not have noticed otherwise. Most students will welcome trying some of these challenges.

9. Circulate around to all the groups, making sure that all students are getting a chance to participate, asking questions to keep the explanatory muscles in their minds working, encouraging them to record their observations, and reminding students to observe safety rules.

Some teachers like adding to the class lists of "What We've Observed About Dry Ice" and "Questions We Have About Dry Ice" at the end of this session, while students are fresh from their explorations. Others prefer not to take exploration time away from the students and do this in subsequent sessions. It's ideal when the recording can happen organically, writing observations and questions down in an ongoing way as they come up rather than having to set aside special times to do it. Plan the times you would like students to add to these lists according to your preferences and your class' cadence. You will need a rich list of questions for Activity 4.

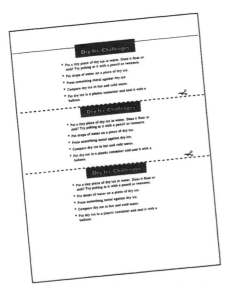

Ending Explorations (for now)

1. Give your students first a 10-minute, and then a 5-minute warning before stopping their explorations. This may not be easy to do! Explain that they will have more opportunities to work with dry ice in upcoming sessions.

2. At the designated stopping time use your usual signal to get their attention (you could tell them to freeze!). Instruct them as to how you would like cleanup to proceed.

3. Tell your students that for homework, you would like them to complete their Dry Ice Explorations sheets, focusing on writing four explanations for four things they tried/observed. They should write their best explanation for what they saw.

Some teachers prefer to do this homework assignment in class in a separate session.

page 1

Team Members: _____

_____

Dry Ice Explorations

Exploration #1:

- What You Did
(Use words and drawings to show what you did.)

- What You Observed
(Use words and drawings to communicate what you observed.)

- Your Explanation
(How can you explain the results?)

© 1999 by The Regents of the University of California, LHS-GEMS. *Dry Ice Investigations*. **May be duplicated for classroom use.**

© 1999 by The Regents of the University of California, LHS-GEMS. *Dry Ice Investigations.* **May be duplicated for classroom use.**

Team Members: _____

_____

Dry Ice Explorations

Exploration #2:

- What You Did
  (Use words and drawings to show what you did.)

- What You Observed
  (Use words and drawings to communicate what you observed.)

- Your Explanation
  (How can you explain the results?)

© 1999 by The Regents of the University of California, LHS-GEMS. *Dry Ice Investigations*. **May be duplicated for classroom use.**

Team Members: _____

_____

Dry Ice Explorations

Exploration #3:

- What You Did
(Use words and drawings to show what you did.)

- What You Observed
(Use words and drawings to communicate what you observed.)

- Your Explanation
(How can you explain the results?)

© 1999 by The Regents of the University of California, LHS-GEMS. *Dry Ice Investigations.* **May be duplicated for classroom use.**

Team Members: _____

_____

Dry Ice Explorations

Exploration #4:

- What You Did
(Use words and drawings to show what you did.)

- What You Observed
(Use words and drawings to communicate what you observed.)

- Your Explanation
(How can you explain the results?)

Dry Ice Challenges

- Put a tiny piece of dry ice in water. Does it float or sink? Try poking at it with a pencil or tweezers.

- Put drops of water on a piece of dry ice.

- Press something metal against dry ice.

- Compare dry ice in hot and cold water.

- Put dry ice in a plastic container and seal it with a balloon.

Dry Ice Challenges

- Put a tiny piece of dry ice in water. Does it float or sink? Try poking at it with a pencil or tweezers.

- Put drops of water on a piece of dry ice.

- Press something metal against dry ice.

- Compare dry ice in hot and cold water.

- Put dry ice in a plastic container and seal it with a balloon.

Dry Ice Challenges

- Put a tiny piece of dry ice in water. Does it float or sink? Try poking at it with a pencil or tweezers.

- Put drops of water on a piece of dry ice.

- Press something metal against dry ice.

- Compare dry ice in hot and cold water.

- Put dry ice in a plastic container and seal it with a balloon.

© 1999 by The Regents of the University of California, LHS-GEMS. *Dry Ice Investigations*. **May be duplicated for classroom use.**

Session 2: Marge's Systematic Observation

This session features an exciting and revealing phenomenon that occurs when dry ice is added to a soap solution—a cup of water with a few drops of liquid dishwashing detergent in it. It bubbles up, creating a huge mass of foam! This phenomenon is ideal in helping accomplish several things:

1) students who have not yet grasped that the solid dry ice is steadily changing to a gas can discover this in a concrete way, as they observe the gas emanating from the dry ice being trapped in the bubbles;

2) the session guides students to construct a correct explanation for this phenomenon (unlike many of the other things they have observed involving dry ice, which require more complex explanations); and

3) the tremendous interest and curiosity generated when student teams explore what happens makes it a natural and involving way to introduce systematic observation.

At the end of the session, the teacher introduces more information related to what the students have directly observed. The concepts and vocabulary of phases and phase change are introduced, and students are led to the realization that unlike most substances, which change from solid to liquid to gas, dry ice changes from solid directly to gas. The teacher ends by revisiting a molecular model of phase change.

Note: Because students will design their own investigations in pairs later in the unit, we suggest that this session be done in pairs as well, with groups of 4–6 students sharing material. If materials are a problem, it could be done in groups of four, with pairs of students recording their own results on the Marge's Systematic Observation student sheet.

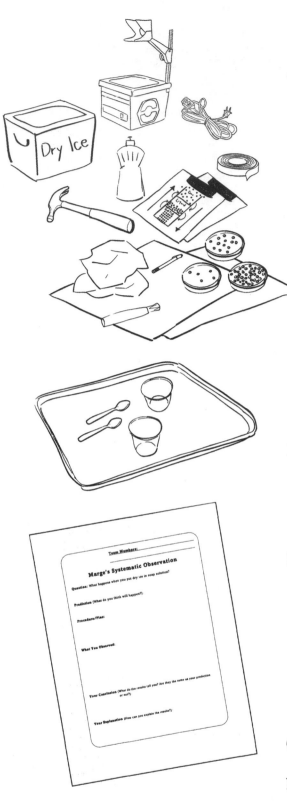

What You Need

For the class:
- ❏ dry ice (about 1 slab)
- ❏ hammer
- ❏ 2 cloths (old T-shirts or T-shirt sized rags)
- ❏ small insulated container for storing pieces of dry ice
- ❏ dishwashing soap
- ❏ an overhead transparency each of the Phase Change Diagram A (master on page 72) and the Phase Change Diagram B (master on page 73)
- ❏ all three BB models (that you made for Activity 1, Session 3)
- ❏ overhead projector
- ❏ extension cord (if needed for overhead projector)
- ❏ an overhead pen
- ❏ 2 pieces of butcher paper
- ❏ 1 marker
- ❏ masking tape

For each group of 4–6 students:
- ❏ 2–3 plastic spoons
- ❏ 2–3 clear plastic cups
- ❏ 1 tray
- ❏ *(optional)* newspapers to cover work surface

For each student:
- ❏ the Scientific Journal (masters at back of guide) or 1 copy of Marge's Systematic Observation student sheet (master on page 71)
- ❏ a pencil
- ❏ *(optional)* 1 copy each of Phase Change Diagrams A and B (masters on pages 72–73) for students to add to their Scientific Journals

Getting Ready

Before the Day of the Activity

1. Plan how you will get dry ice. (See the section entitled "Obtaining and Maintaining Dry Ice" on page 7.) This session requires about one slab of dry ice for a class of 32 students.

2. Acquire the remaining materials needed for this session.

3. Make overhead transparencies of the Phase Change Diagram A (master on page 72) and Phase Change Diagram B (master on page 73).

4. Duplicate student sheets as necessary (masters on pages 71–73).

5. Write the definitions for a variable and a systematic observation on separate pieces of butcher paper for posting later in the session. A *variable* is something which can vary each time you do something. In a *systematic observation*, you make a plan, decide on the conditions, follow the plan, and then carefully observe and record what happens over time.

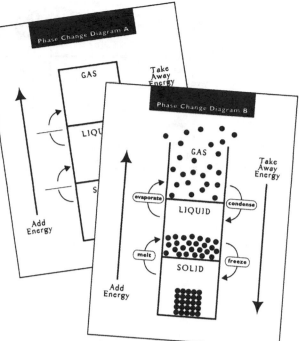

On the Day of the Activity

1. Set up one tray for each group of 4–6 students. On each tray place 2–3 plastic cups and 2–3 plastic spoons.

2. Fill cups half full of water. Add six to eight drops of dishwashing soap to each cup. Stir the mixture.

3. Set up the overhead projector and place the two overhead transparencies, the overhead pen, and the BB models near by.

4. If you are using Scientific Journals, have them on hand or prepare to distribute the appropriate pages depending on how you are managing the journal.

Immediately Before Class

Lay a slab of dry ice on a towel, T-shirt, or other rag. Place another towel or cloth on top of it. Use the side of a hammer to break the dry ice through the rag, into small pieces. Put the broken pieces in a small insulated container.

Important Note: For this activity, we've found that the bubbling up phenomenon is most impressive when the piece of dry ice used is about 1 ½" in diameter and there is sufficient water (with soap drops) in the cup to fully submerge the piece of dry ice.

Sharing Explanations

1. Ask students to take out the Dry Ice Explorations sheet they worked on for homework. Take just a few minutes to ask students for observations and explanations about dry ice they made during the last session. Ask several volunteers to share.

2. Choose a common observation that was shared and ask if anyone else had a different explanation for the same observation. Try to elicit several different explanations for the same observation.

3. Conclude by saying that this is what leads scientists to design scientific tests and experiments—to answer questions they have. Sometimes they can't get the answer after a day of trying things, observing, or experimenting. Sometimes it takes weeks or even years to come up with an accurate explanation. First explanations are good, because they help us ask the next question. The best explanations are the ones that get refined to reflect new information.

4. Take just a few minutes to have the class add more questions to the class list of "Questions We Have About Dry Ice."

Introducing Systematic Observation

1. Write the question, "What happens when you put dry ice in soap solution?" on the board, and tell the class that today they are going to try and find the answer to that question.

2. Ask students for their predictions about what will happen when dry ice is added to a soap solution. Explain that scientists also make predictions about what they think will happen. Write "Prediction" on the board. Record a few student predictions about what might happen.

3. Ask how we could find out the answer to the question. Students will probably blurt out the obvious—put some dry ice in soap solution and watch! Ask them the following questions to raise awareness about variables and the importance of a well-thought-out plan or procedure. Write the bold phrase on the chalkboard as you ask each question.

- Do you think it matters **how much dry ice** we use?
- Does it matter **how much soap solution** we use?
- Does it matter **when the dry ice is added** to the soap solution?
- Does it matter **what kind of a container** we use?

4. Tell them that these things which can *vary,* or change, each time you do something are called *variables.* Write the heading "Variables" over the list of bold phrases. Post the butcher paper with the definition of a variable.

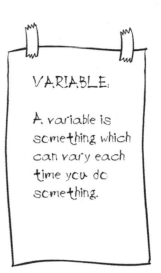

VARIABLE:

A variable is something which can vary each time you do something.

5. Conclude by saying that scientists make a plan for each of these variables. Explain that the class will have one plan for everyone to follow. Start by showing them the container you have for them to use (the plastic cup). Let the students know that you have already filled the cups half full of water, added 6–8 drops of dishwashing soap and stirred the mixture. Also let them know that they'll use a piece of dry ice about 1 ½" in diameter that will be completely submerged in the water.

6. Point out that what they'll be doing is a more **systematic** way of observing than what they have done so far in this unit. Up until now, their observations have been focused on what they observe about things. Today they have a question they want to answer (What happens when you put dry ice in soap solution?), they made a plan for a situation they would like to observe (putting dry ice in soap solution), they have set up the conditions for the situation they want (putting a certain size chunk of dry ice in a certain amount of soap solution in a certain way), they made a prediction, and then they will carefully observe over time as they follow their plan. This is called a *systematic observation.* Post the butcher paper with the definition of a systematic observation.

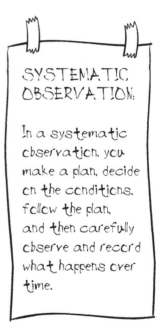

SYSTEMATIC OBSERVATION:

In a systematic observation, you make a plan, decide on the conditions, follow the plan, and then carefully observe and record what happens over time.

7. Tell them that after they conduct their systematic observation, you'd like them to record their observations and explanations for what happened on page 7 of their Scientific Journals, or on a sheet that you will distribute. Remind them that they should not worry about whether or not they think their explanation is "the right answer," but try to make sure it reflects the results they observed.

Systematic Observation (or Marge Simpson's Hairdo!)

1. Distribute the materials so each pair has a cup with soap solution and a spoon. You may want to have students put newspaper underneath the work area to help minimize the mess.

2. Distribute the dry ice, Scientific Journals (ask students to turn to page 7) or Marge's Systematic Observation student sheets, and have students begin.

3. Circulate as students observe what happens. Let them observe and marvel at what is taking place for an initial period. Then keep circulating, asking questions to spur their thinking, and reminding them to record observations and begin to discuss their explanations.

4. When they've finished, have students return all the materials to a central location, following your clean up instructions. Then focus their attention for a discussion of what they've just experienced.

Bubbling Up with Explanations

1. Facilitate a discussion of what they've just observed, with emphasis on possible explanations. Once again, and as needed, emphasize that they should stretch their minds to come up with possible explanations and not be worried about the exact right answer.

2. Ask questions to encourage their thought process:

* Can you describe exactly what happened?

* Why do you think this is happening? There's nobody standing there blowing bubbles—what's going on?

* Does dry ice always form bubbles?

* What do you think is making the bubbles?

* What is inside the bubbles and where did it come from?

* Are the bubbles the same or different from soap bubbles blown by people?

- What makes these bubbles cloudy?

- Can you explain what happened?

3. If your students do not already suggest it (or have not already done so previously) introduce the idea that dry ice gives off a *gas*. That's what is filling the bubbles. (In fact, the bubbles are spheres of soap solution that have gas inside.) Explain that when the solid dry ice is dropped into soapy water, it immediately starts producing gas. The gas inflates the soap film just like our breath blows up a bubble in a bubble-blower, and that's why lots and lots of bubbles start to form.

4. You may want to remind them of their comparisons between water ice and dry ice. Point out that dry ice is called "dry" ice because, unlike frozen water ice, it does not "melt" into a liquid. Ask, "What happens to it?" [it turns directly into a gas]

5. Ask, "What happens to regular ice when it is heated?" [It first melts into a liquid, then, when enough heat is added, it turns into steam, or water vapor.] Reiterate that water goes through the stage of being a liquid before it becomes a gas.

Introducing Phases and Phase Changes

1. Turn on the overhead projector. Show the transparency of the Phase Change Diagram A.

   a. Discuss the typical phase changes that occur when you add energy (heat) to matter—**solid to liquid to gas.** Ask your students to describe what happens and, if they don't use the terms, add the vocabulary we use for these changes to the chart (**melting** and **evaporation**).

   b. Show the typical phase changes that occur when you take energy away from matter (cool it down)—**gas to liquid to solid.** Ask your students to describe what happens and, if they don't use the terms, add the vocabulary we use for these changes to the chart (**condensation** and **freezing**).

   c. Use an overhead pen to show how dry ice does not follow the typical phase change sequence. It skips the liquid phase and goes directly from a solid to a gas when energy is added and gas to solid when energy is

If your students are fans of "The Simpsons" on TV, you may want to add that the phenomenon they observed today has been compared to Marge Simpson's beehive hairstyle!

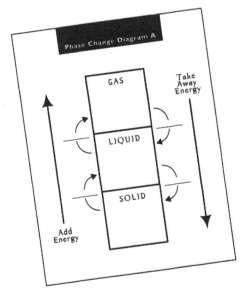

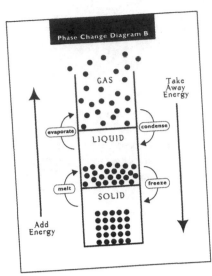

Phase Change Diagram B

*Depending on your students' age and prior knowledge you may also want to introduce or reinforce the terminology of "phases" and "phase change." A substance can be in a solid, liquid, or gaseous form. Whenever a substance changes from one form to another it is undergoing a **phase change**. At room temperature and standard atmospheric pressure, dry ice undergoes a phase change (it turns into a gas), as does water ice (it melts into a liquid), as do a number of other substances. Under the appropriate conditions, dry ice will also liquefy, but this can only take place at 5 times standard atmospheric pressure.*

taken away. Draw arrows on the diagram indicating that. That process is called **sublimation.** Write the word sublimation on the transparency.

2. Show the transparency of the Phase Change Diagram B. Tell the class that we are going to again pretend that we can see molecules and see what matter would look like.

    a. Remind them (or ask them to recall) that molecules of water (H_2O) themselves stay the same when energy is added—they just move faster and farther apart.

    b. Point out that the same is true for dry ice. Ask students if they remember what dry ice is made of. [carbon dioxide—CO_2] Ask them what gas is emitted from dry ice. [carbon dioxide]

3. Use all three BB models (of a solid, a liquid, and a gas) to quickly go through the phases. Put the solid model on the overhead and wiggle it so the BBs vibrate. Then quickly replace it with the liquid model and move the dish faster so the BBs appear to move "fluidly." Then quickly replace it with the gas model and move the dish back and forth quickly so the BBs appear as a blur. Do this several times, from solid to liquid to gas to liquid to solid, each time saying the names of the phases, and using the phase change vocabulary (melting, evaporating, condensing, freezing).

4. Do it one last time, but this time with just the solid and gas models—representing sublimation. Show how dry ice goes from a solid to a gas.

5. If you have decided to use them, distribute the Phase Change Diagrams A and B for each student to add to their journal.

Marge's Systematic Observation

Question: What happens when you put dry ice in soap solution?

Prediction (What do you think will happen?):

Procedure/Plan:

What You Observed:

Your Conclusion (What do the results tell you? Are they the same as your prediction or not?):

Your Explanation (How can you explain the results?):

© 1999 by The Regents of the University of California, LHS-GEMS. *Dry Ice Investigations.* **May be duplicated for classroom use.**

Phase Change Diagram A

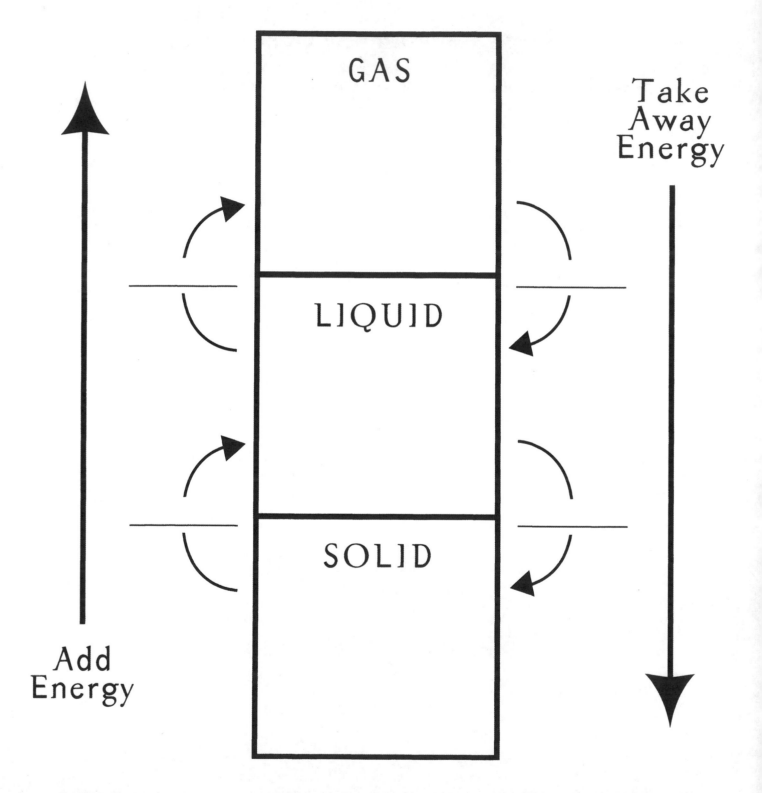

GAS

LIQUID

SOLID

Add Energy

Take Away Energy

© 1999 by The Regents of the University of California, LHS-GEMS. *Dry Ice Investigations*. **May be duplicated for classroom use.**

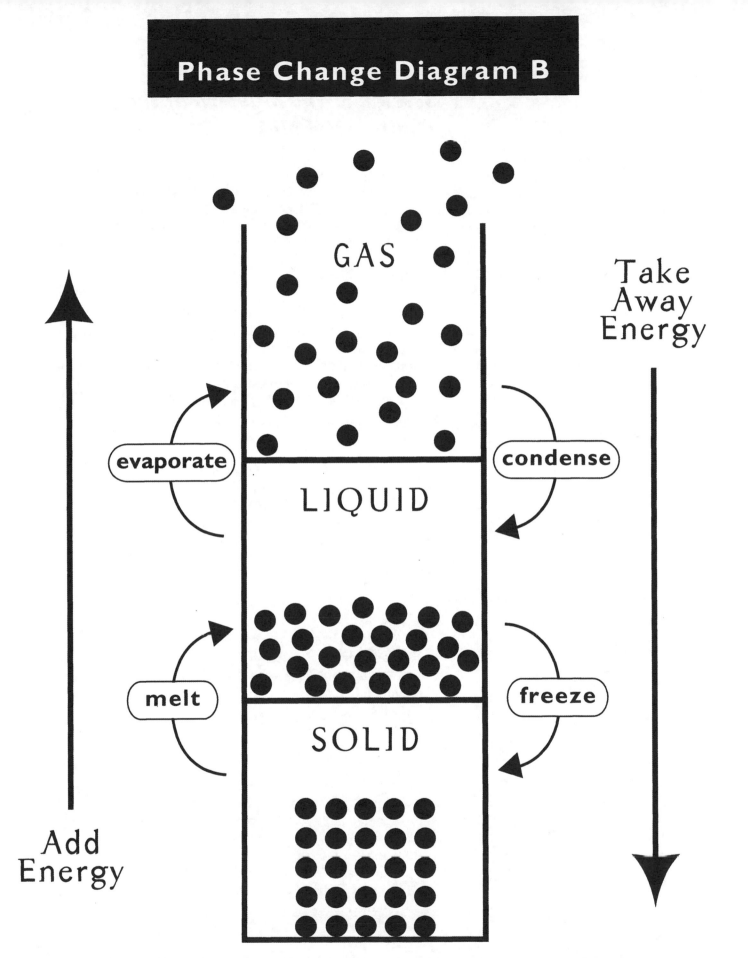

Phase Change Diagram B

GAS

Add Energy

Take Away Energy

evaporate

condense

LIQUID

melt

freeze

SOLID

© 1999 by The Regents of the University of California, LHS-GEMS. *Dry Ice Investigations.* **May be duplicated for classroom use.**

Session 3: The Mystery of the Floating Bubbles

In this session, the class conducts another systematic observation. The teacher blows several soap bubbles and the students watch as they descend into an aquarium whose bottom is lined with dry ice. The bubbles descend to a certain level and then stop, mysteriously floating inside the aquarium. What could explain the mystery of the floating bubbles?

Students apply their knowledge of dry ice as they attempt to explain why the bubbles float. First working in pairs, and then in the whole group, students suggest various explanations and further questions they have. The teacher poses a series of questions that guide the class to an understanding of the phenomenon—that the bubbles are floating on a layer of (heavy/dense) carbon dioxide gas.

What evidence could they get to confirm or modify this explanation? The teacher tests the gas in the aquarium with a lighted match. The match goes out, confirming the fact there is no air (oxygen) left in the bottom of the container; it is filled with a layer of carbon dioxide gas.

What You Need

For the class:
- ❏ dry ice (½ to 1 cup of dry ice pieces)
- ❏ hammer
- ❏ 2 cloths (old T-shirts or T-shirt sized rags)
- ❏ small insulated container for storing pieces of dry ice
- ❏ dishwashing soap

For the demonstration:
- ❏ cup with small amount of bubble solution or diluted liquid dishwashing soap (approximately 2 tablespoons of soap in 1 cup of water)
- ❏ about 5 straws or a few bubble blowers
- ❏ 1 high-sided transparent container, such as an empty aquarium or a large (5 gallon) heavy-duty glass cylindrical container (See "Getting Ready" for details.)
- ❏ matches

For each student:
- ❏ the Scientific Journal (masters at back of guide) or 1 copy of the Mystery of the Floating Bubbles student sheet (master on page 80)
- ❏ a pencil

Getting Ready

Before the Day of the Activity

1. Plan how you will get dry ice. (See the section entitled "Obtaining and Maintaining Dry Ice" on page 7.)

2. Obtain a transparent high-sided wide container, such as an aquarium, for the demonstration. A dishtub or other similar container (without transparent sides) can be substituted, but this will create a problem for you to solve. (See below.) In order for the demonstration to work, the container must have high enough sides to contain a volume of "dry ice gas" and its top opening must be wide enough so that you can successfully float a soap bubble into it and then watch it descend to the bottom of the container. (Narrow containers make this difficult—the soap bubble hits the side before descending to the bottom of the container.)

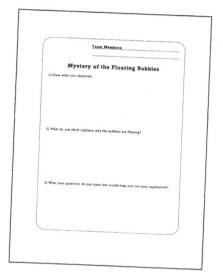

If your container does not have transparent sides, it can work, but it will be difficult for the entire class to see the demonstration at the same time from their seats. Some teachers have found a way to situate the container (low down) and the students (all around) so that all can see. Other teachers have asked an adult volunteer to come to class and conduct the demonstration at a side table for each small group, throughout the class session, while the other students do something else. While many of these solutions have worked, we recommend that it will be easiest for you to work extra hard to borrow an aquarium or other large transparent high-sided container.

3. Acquire the remaining materials needed for this session.

4. Duplicate student sheets as necessary (master on page 80).

On the Day of the Activity

1. If you are using Scientific Journals, have them on hand or prepare to distribute the appropriate pages depending on how you are managing the journal.

2. Set out the materials for the demonstration in a central location.

Immediately Before Class

1. Lay a slab of dry ice on a towel, T-shirt, or other rag. Place another towel or cloth on top of it. Use the side of a hammer to break the dry ice through the rag. Put the broken pieces in a small insulated container.

2. Put most of the cup of dry ice in the bottom of the aquarium. More is better if you have dry ice to spare.

Floating Bubbles Demonstration

1. Ask the class a few questions to review what we know about dry ice so far:

- What is dry ice made of? [carbon dioxide]

- What happens to solid dry ice at room temperature? [it changes to a gas—it sublimes]

- Are the molecules in "solid dry ice" different from the molecules in "dry ice gas?" [no, they're just moving faster and farther apart in the gas]

- What makes the solid carbon dioxide change to gaseous carbon dioxide? [energy; heat]

2. Tell the class that today they are going to do another systematic observation with dry ice. Explain that you will do a demonstration, several times. You'd like them to carefully observe what happens. Then you would like them to work in pairs to discuss a possible explanation for what is occurring.

3. Tell them that you will blow a soap bubble and let it float down into the aquarium containing the dry ice. Ask for predictions of what might happen. It may take a

minute or two for the carbon dioxide gas layer to build up. Then go ahead and add the bubbles:

- Dip a straw or other bubble blowing device in the solution and gently blow a bubble in the air **above** the aquarium, so the bubble **floats** down into the aquarium. This will probably take a few tries. The first bubble might sink quickly as it often has a drop of bubble solution on it that makes it heavier. Try blowing a second bubble without redipping your straw. Be sure **not to blow into** the aquarium, or else the dry ice gas will be blown out of the aquarium.

Students should observe that the bubbles float on the layer of carbon dioxide gas, created by the subliming dry ice. **Note:** Do not tell students why the bubbles float. That's the mystery for them to solve! If the bubbles are very small, they are less likely to float. Hint for making larger bubbles: If you are using a straw to blow bubbles, blow more slowly, then flick them off the straw.

4. After several minutes of observing, ask for observations of what's happening. Call on several volunteers.

5. Distribute the Scientific Journals (ask students to turn to page 8) or the Mystery of the Floating Bubbles student sheets to pairs of students and challenge them to come up with **explanations** for this phenomenon.

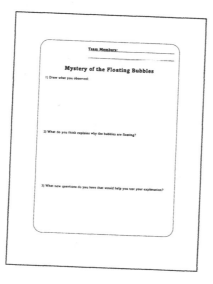

If you have trouble observing the floating bubbles phenomenon it may be because the invisible layer of carbon dioxide gas has not accumulated in the aquarium. Try one or more of the following things: Add more dry ice to the bottom of the aquarium. Break up the dry ice into smaller pieces. As a last resort, you can add some water to the dry ice to increase the rate at which it sublimes. The problem with this is that too much fog may form, making it hard for students to see.

Explaining the Mystery of the Floating Bubbles

1. Circulate as student pairs discuss their ideas. Ask probing questions. Encourage students to generate their own new questions that could help them confirm their explanations.

2. When most students have completed their student sheets, regain the attention of the entire class.

3. Ask one pair to share their explanation, and what further questions they have that would help them confirm that their explanation is correct. Record what they say on the board. Ask for hands of those who came up with a similar explanation.

4. Ask a pair with a different explanation to share what they think, and what further questions they came up with. Record this second explanation on the board. Poll others who chose the same explanation. Add one or two more explanations depending on student interest.

5. Lead a discussion with the class to help them explain the mystery. If students are at a loss, use questions like the following to guide the discussion. The goal is not a lock-step question/answer sequence, but a thoughtful discussion, driven by questions. These questions are meant to help you facilitate your class' unique discussion.

- What was in the container before we put the dry ice in? [air]

- What was in the container after we added the dry ice and hot water? [air, dry ice, water, and carbon dioxide gas]

If students don't say carbon dioxide gas, ask:

- What happens to dry ice when you add energy (heat)? [the solid carbon dioxide changes to gaseous carbon dioxide]

- Why do you think the bubble appears to float at this level in the container?

- What invisible substance might have filled the bottom part of the container?

- The cold from the ice keeps the bubbles from sinking.
    If we blew a bubble in a cold room, would it sink?

- The gas from the dry ice forms a layer and the bubbles sit on that layer.
    Could we test for CO_2 gas?

- What can we say about carbon dioxide gas compared to air? [It's heavier—more dense. That's why the carbon dioxide gas accumulates at the bottom of the container.]

- What can we say about the soap bubbles I blew? [They're lighter—less dense than carbon dioxide gas. That's why they float on the layer of carbon dioxide gas.]

- What evidence might we be able to collect that supports our explanation—that the bubble is floating on a layer of carbon dioxide gas? [maybe there's a test for carbon dioxide gas]

6. Explain that pure carbon dioxide gas will not support a flame. Oxygen gas is required in order for fire to burn. Ask students how they could use this information to answer the question of what gas might be in the container.

7. Accept several suggestions. Summarize by saying that you can test one of the properties of the gases in the container to see if there **is** an area with no oxygen (therefore no air). If you have time, you might want to try one or more of the students' suggestions. Otherwise, allow the group to agree on one thing they might like to try.

8. If you have run out of time, just light a match and slowly lower it into the container. Let the students observe that the match goes out when it hits the layer of carbon dioxide gas. Conclude by saying that this test provides more evidence that there is indeed a layer of pure carbon dioxide gas at the bottom of the container.

9. Point out that making careful, systematic observations (like they did of the floating bubbles demonstration) often leads to more questions. Sometimes we can think of tests or experiments to answer those questions; sometimes they are hard to answer.

10. Ask the class for additional questions about dry ice that they now have and add them to the class list of questions.

Some students may say that human breath is CO_2, which it partly is, although it is mostly nitrogen.

Occasionally, students may see a bubble slowly sink and get bigger— this is due to carbon dioxide gas penetrating through the bubble wall.

One class decided to place three lighted candles of different heights in holders in the bottom of an empty aquarium. They then carefully added dry ice and hot water and watched as the candles went out, shortest to tallest.

Team Members:
_____

_____

Mystery of the Floating Bubbles

1) Draw what you observed:

2) What do you think explains why the bubbles are floating?

3) What new questions do you have that would help you test your explanation?

© 1999 by The Regents of the University of California, LHS-GEMS. *Dry Ice Investigations*. **May be duplicated for classroom use.**

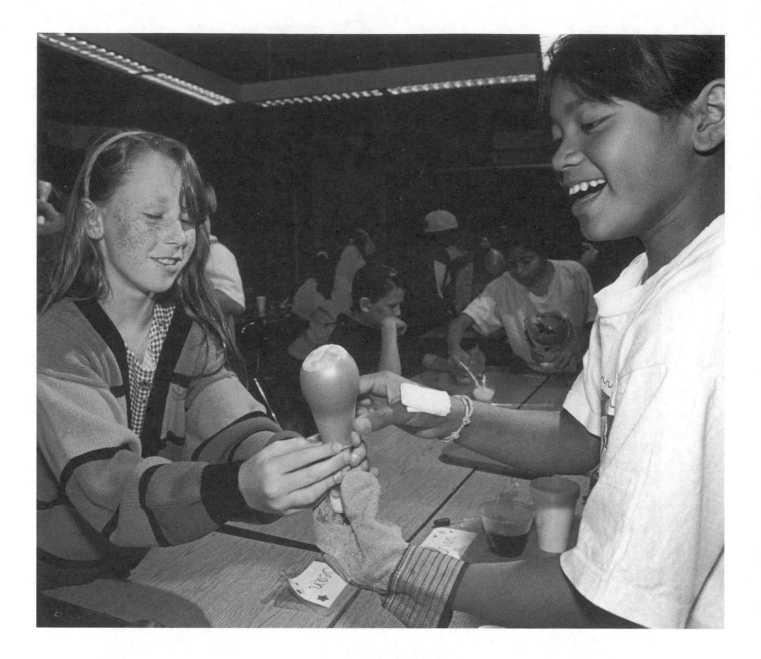

Activity 3: Experimenting

Overview

In this one-session activity, students are guided through conducting an experiment. The experiment is designed to determine whether temperature affects the rate of sublimation of dry ice. Students do a variation on one of the systematic observations (Marge Simpson's Hairdo) they conducted in the last activity. However this time they do it as an experiment—by setting up a comparison of two situations that are alike in every way but one (temperature).

This time, the experiment they conduct is planned for them, with the goal of helping them distinguish between systematic observations (that have no comparison groups) and experiments (that have "controls" or comparison groups). This experience will prepare students for later in the unit when they will have the opportunity to design and conduct their own investigations (choosing either a systematic observation or setting up an experiment).

After conducting the experiment, students are challenged to draw a conclusion—that more heat (energy) causes dry ice to sublimate faster. Then they are challenged to repeat the experiment and find a way to quantify their conclusion. Some students choose to compare the height of soap bubble columns that are formed, others might compare the time it takes for the mass of bubbles to hit the table, still others might compare the size of the individual bubbles. Students gain insight and practice into an important part of designing experiments—determining a measure of the "outcome variable."

The objectives of this activity are to: distinguish between systematic observations and experiments; introduce the concept of test and outcome variables; be guided through an experiment; practice drawing conclusions; gain experience determining the outcome variable and how to quantify results; and to discover that increased energy increases the rate of sublimation.

Note: As mentioned previously, because students will design their own investigations in pairs later in the unit, we suggest that this session be done in pairs as well. Materials can be shared among groups of 4–6 students.

Session 1: Marge's Experiments

What You Need

For the class:
- ❏ dry ice (about 1 slab)
- ❏ hammer
- ❏ 2 cloths (old T-shirts or T-shirt sized rags)
- ❏ small insulated container for storing pieces of dry ice
- ❏ dishwashing soap
- ❏ 1 cold water dispenser, such as a dishtub or cooler (sending kids to the sink can work too, if you have water in your classroom)
- ❏ 1 hot water dispenser (such as an electric coffee maker)
- ❏ 3 pieces of butcher paper
- ❏ 1 marker
- ❏ masking tape

For each group of 4–6 students:
- ❏ 2–3 plastic spoons
- ❏ 8–12 clear plastic cups
- ❏ 1 tray
- ❏ *(optional)* newspapers to cover work surface

For each student:
- ❏ the Scientific Journal (masters at back of guide) or 1 copy each of Marge's Experiment: Take 1 and Marge's Experiment: Take 2 student sheets (masters on pages 90–91)
- ❏ a pencil

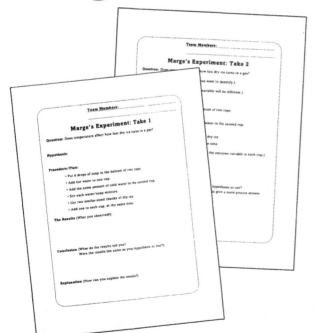

Getting Ready

Before the Day of the Activity

1. Plan how you will get dry ice. (See the section entitled "Obtaining and Maintaining Dry Ice" on page 7.) This session requires about one slab of dry ice for a class of 32 students.

2. Obtain hot and cold water dispensers. Students will need a way to access hot and cold water for their experi-

ments. The water needn't be very hot or very cold, but different enough in temperature so that students can test the effect of this variable. An electric coffee pot or an "air pot" work particularly well as hot water dispensers because of the easy and safe way students can dispense the water (with a spigot or by pressing a button). Other large insulated thermos-type containers can work well too.

3. Acquire the remaining materials needed for this session.

4. Duplicate student sheets as necessary (masters on pages 90–91).

5. Write the definitions for an experiment, a test variable, and an outcome variable on separate pieces of butcher paper for posting later in the session. In an *experiment*, you make a comparison between two situations, keeping all things the same except one. A *test variable* is the one thing you plan to be different in an experiment. An *outcome variable* is the result you compare in an experiment.

On the Day of the Activity

1. Set up one tray for each group of 4–6 students. On each tray place 8–12 plastic cups and 2–3 plastic spoons.

2. Add six drops of dishwashing soap to each cup.

3. In a central location, place the following materials: hot water dispenser, cold water dispenser, and broken pieces of dry ice in an insulated container (see below).

4. If you are using Scientific Journals, have them on hand or prepare to distribute the appropriate pages depending on how you are managing the journal.

Immediately Before Class

1. Lay a slab of dry ice on a towel, T-shirt, or other rag. Place another towel or cloth on top of it. Use the side of a hammer to break the dry ice through the rag. Put the broken pieces in a small insulated container.

2. Fill and plug in the hot water heater (or heat water to fill your insulated hot water dispenser).

Setting up an Experiment

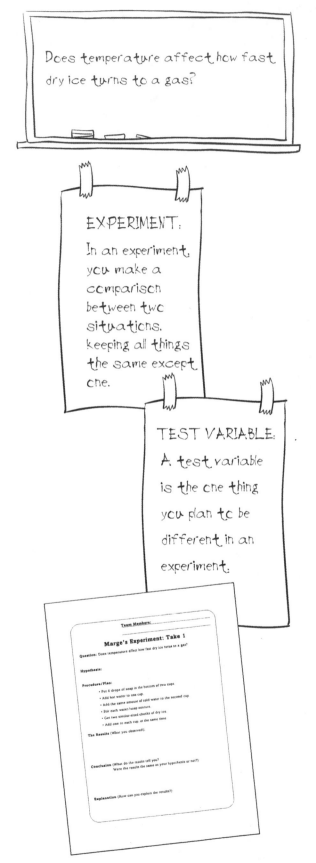

Does temperature affect how fast dry ice turns to a gas?

EXPERIMENT:

In an experiment, you make a comparison between two situations, keeping all things the same except one.

TEST VARIABLE:

A test variable is the one thing you plan to be different in an experiment.

Team Members:

Marge's Experiment: Take 1

Question: Does temperature affect how fast dry ice turns to a gas?

Hypothesis:

Procedure/Plan:
- Put 6 drops of soap in the bottom of two cups
- Add hot water to one cup
- Add the same amount of cold water to the second cup
- Stir each water/soap mixture.
- Get two similar-sized chunks of dry ice.
- Add one to each cup, at the same time

The Results (What you observed):

Conclusion (What do the results tell you?)
Were the results the same as your hypothesis or not?)

Explanation (How can you explain the results?)

1. Remind the students that the other day, they conducted a systematic observation to answer the question, "What happens when you put dry ice in soap solution?" Ask the class to recall the answer to the question. [it makes a tower of foam] Ask, "What creates the foam?" [the carbon dioxide gas from the dry ice] Remind them that this was a systematic observation, because they made a plan (to add dry ice to soap solution), controlled the conditions, followed the plan, and then carefully observed what happened over time.

2. Tell them that today, you have another question for them to answer, "Does temperature affect how fast dry ice turns to a gas?" Depending on the experience of your students, you might want to explain that another way of asking that same thing is "Does temperature affect the rate at which dry ice sublimates?" Write the appropriate question on the board.

3. Ask for ideas for how they could answer that question. Accept several ideas. Let students know that while there are many different ways to go about answering the question, the best ways all compare two things that are alike in all ways except one. Ask what one thing should be different. [temperature]

4. Explain that when you make a comparison between two situations like this, where all things are the same except one, it is called an *experiment.* When you plan an experiment you keep all variables the same, except one. The one thing that you "vary" is called the ***test variable.*** Post the pieces of butcher paper with the definitions of an experiment and a test variable.

5. Say that, just as for a systematic observations, you also need a carefully thought-out plan for an experiment. Explain that while there are many ways to conduct an experiment that can answer the question of whether temperature affects the rate at which dry ice sublimates, you are going to ask that they all follow the same plan today. Distribute Marge's Experiment: Take 1 student sheets or instruct them to turn to page 9 in their Scientific Journals so they can follow along with the plan.

6. Present the plan, using the materials as props as necessary:

- Put 6 drops of dishwashing soap in the bottom of two cups. (Point out that you have done this for them.)

- Add the same amount of water to each cup; one cup should have hot water, the other cup should have cold water. (Remind them how to safely get water from the hot and cold water dispensers you have set up. Emphasize that they should put **the same amount** of water in each cup.)

- Stir each water/soap mixture.

- Get two similar-sized chunks of dry ice. At the same time, put the two pieces of dry ice into the two cups of water. (Ideally, these should be weighed to be exactly the same. If classroom conditions do not allow this, an approximation is acceptable.)

7. Summarize by saying that everything (all variables) should be the same in the two cups except the temperature of water (the test variable). Tell students these final steps they should follow to complete the experiment.

- After the dry ice is put in the soap solutions of different temperatures, carefully observe over time and compare what's happening in the two cups.

- After a few minutes, draw your own conclusion about the results of your experiment to answer the question.

8. Ask if there are any questions about what they are to do.

9. Ask students for their predictions about what will happen. Accept a few.

10. Remind them to record their hypothesis (a proposed explanation for what is going to happen), observations, conclusion, and explanation for what happened on page 9 of their Scientific Journal or on the student sheet.

*You may want to discuss the meaning of "hypothesis." An **hypothesis** is a statement given as an explanation for something that happens. It can be a working hypothesis, as in this case—an explanation to guide an investigation. Or it can be a more established statement, accepted as highly probable based on already established experiments or facts. Hypotheses are sometimes considered to be predictions, but scientifically speaking should include a proposed explanation to be a true hypothesis. Some teachers ask students to frame their hypothesis as an "if...then..." statement that tells the relationship between the variables.*

Conducting the Experiment

1. Tell the students that they will be working in pairs. Ask a volunteer from each group of four to get a tray of equipment for pairs to share. You may want to have students put newspaper underneath the work area to help minimize the mess.

2. After students have put hot and cold water in their cups, walk around to each table group, distributing chunks of dry ice for them to use.

3. Circulate to assist students as needed. Encourage them to record their hypothesis, observations, conclusion, and explanation. Also, enforce safety rules.

Refining the Experiment

1. When all pairs are mostly finished, get the attention of the class. (This might require that you collect the cups filled with bubbles—they won't need them again.) Ask if they know the answer to the original question: "Does temperature affect how fast dry ice turns to a gas?" Ask each group to explain how they knew.

2. Point out that different groups of students compared different indicators or variables in drawing their conclusions about the affect of temperature on dry ice. Give examples of some of the variables that groups used. Say that sometimes scientists compare one variable to draw their conclusions, sometimes they compare more than one variable. The variables that they compare are sometimes called *outcome variables.* Post the butcher paper with the definition of an outcome variable.

3. Explain that scientists often want to quantify the results of an experiment. They find some way to count or measure an outcome variable. Ask for ideas how they could do this.

4. Tell students they will now repeat the experiment, but this time to find a quantitative way to compare or measure the outcome variable that they use. Distribute Marge's Experiment: Take 2 student sheets or instruct them to turn to page 10 in their Scientific Journals. Encourage them to record their method of quantifying their results.

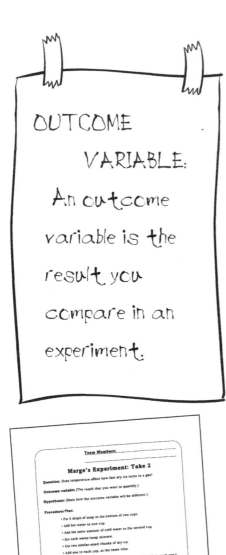

OUTCOME VARIABLE: An outcome variable is the result you compare in an experiment.

Team Members:

Marge's Experiment: Take 2

Question: Does temperature affect how fast dry ice turns to a gas?

Outcome variable (The result that you want to quantify.):

Hypothesis: (State how the outcome variable will be different.)

Procedure/Plan:
- Put 5 drops of soap in the bottom of two cups
- Add hot water to one cup.
- Add the same amount of cold water to the second cup
- Stir each water/soap mixture.
- Get two similar-sized chunks of dry ice
- Add one to each cup, at the same time.

The Results (What you observed! Compare the outcome variable in each cup.):

Conclusion (What do the results tell you?
Were the results the same as your hypothesis or not?
Did having a way to measure results give a more precise answer to the question?):

Explanation (How can you explain the results?):

5. After students have filled their second set of cups with hot and cold water and stirred each water/soap mixture, walk around to each group with the dry ice. Check that a pair has come up with one way to quantitatively compare the results of the experiment (size of bubble, height of bubble mass, time it takes for bubble mass to hit table, etc.) before distributing chunks of dry ice for them to use.

6. When the pairs have finished, have them return all the materials to a central location, following your clean up instructions. Then focus their attention for a quick debrief of the methods different students used to quantify the results of their experiment.

7. Make a list of several different quantification methods on the board. Facilitate a discussion of the problems and surprises they encountered.

Dry ice Limericks   Emily Greenberger
                           Nov-12-917
                           Science 6B

I put dry ice in plastic.
The gas it made was fantastic.
The gas over loaded
the bag exploded.
The result my dear was
quite drastic.

In science we studied dry ice
Our directions were very precise.
One little touch,
the burn would be such.
You'd want to go back to wet ice.

Team Members:

Marge's Experiment: Take 1

Question: Does temperature affect how fast dry ice turns to a gas?

Hypothesis:

Procedure/Plan:

- Put 6 drops of soap in the bottom of two cups.

- Add hot water to one cup.

- Add the same amount of cold water to the second cup.

- Stir each water/soap mixture.

- Get two similar-sized chunks of dry ice.

- Add one to each cup, at the same time.

The Results (What you observed!):

Conclusion (What do the results tell you?
Were the results the same as your hypothesis or not?):

Explanation (How can you explain the results?):

© 1999 by The Regents of the University of California, LHS-GEMS. *Dry Ice Investigations.* May be duplicated for classroom use.

_____

Marge's Experiment: Take 2

Question: Does temperature affect how fast dry ice turns to a gas?

Outcome variable (The result that you want to quantify.):

Hypothesis: (State how the outcome variable will be different.):

Procedure/Plan:

- Put 6 drops of soap in the bottom of two cups.
- Add hot water to one cup.
- Add the same amount of cold water to the second cup.
- Stir each water/soap mixture.
- Get two similar-sized chunks of dry ice.
- Add one to each cup, at the same time.

The Results (What you observed! Compare the outcome variable in each cup.):

Conclusion (What do the results tell you?
Were the results the same as your hypothesis or not?
Did having a way to measure results give a more precise answer
to the question?):

Explanation (How can you explain the results?):

© 1999 by The Regents of the University of California, LHS-GEMS. *Dry Ice Investigations.* **May be duplicated for classroom use.**

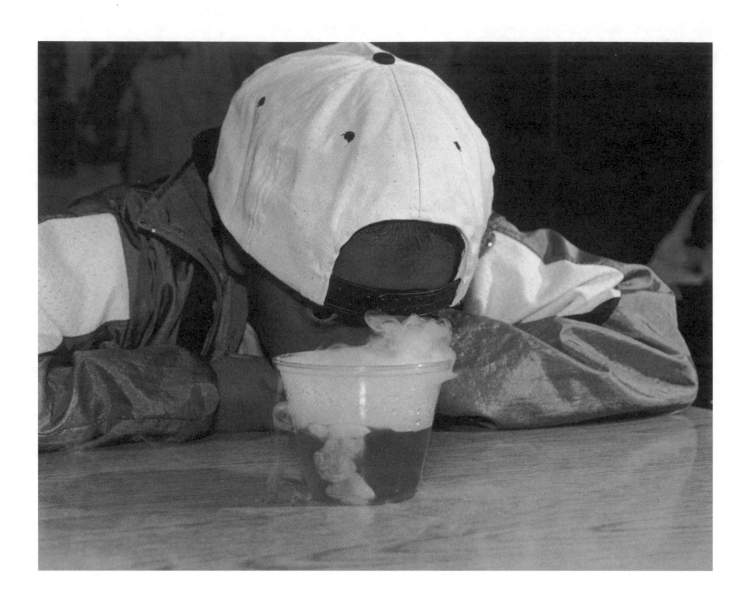

Activity 4: Conducting Dry Ice Investigations

Overview

This four-session activity is in many ways the culmination of the *Dry Ice Investigations* unit. In previous activities, students have practiced various elements of investigation in the context of guided-inquiry activities. In this activity, students plan and conduct their own investigations in a more open-ended way.

In Sessions 1 and 2, the teacher provides the "scaffolding" to assist students in planning successful investigations. In Session 1, pairs of students choose their own investigable questions and the kind of investigation they plan to design; in Session 2, students make their investigation plans. In Session 3, pairs of students conduct their investigations, refine them, and then conduct them again. Students are given the rubric with which their investigations will be evaluated and use this to guide their work. In Session 4, the teacher chooses one of several methods for having students share the results of their investigations.

The objectives of this activity are to: gain experience distinguishing between investigable questions and non-investigable questions; choose whether a systematic observation or an experiment is best to answer a particular question; plan the details of an investigation, controlling variables and/or identifying outcome variables as appropriate; conduct and refine the investigation making adjustments as necessary, and use careful reasoning to make sense of the data and draw conclusions.

Session 1: Choosing Investigable Questions

Students begin by focusing on the class list of questions about dry ice that has been generated over the course of the unit, and are told that they will get to choose a question that interests them for further investigation. Students focus on distinguishing investigable questions from non-investigable questions through a sorting activity and a class discussion of the results. They also discuss what kinds of questions are best investigated by doing a systematic observation and what kinds are best investigated by doing an experiment.

Students are then given a rubric for evaluating investigations. They use this as they choose and frame their own investigation questions and decide whether they will design a systematic observation or an experiment. Finally, pairs of students critique each other's questions and investigation decisions using the rubric.

What You Need

For the class:

❏ class list of "Questions We Have About Dry Ice" (generated throughout the unit)
❏ an overhead transparency each of Planning Our Investigation (first page only; master on page 108), Sorting Questions 1 (master on page 112), Sorting Questions 2 (master on page 113), and Question Strips (front side only; master on page 114)
❏ overhead projector
❏ extension cord (if needed for overhead projector)
❏ an overhead pen
❏ 1 piece of butcher paper
❏ 1 marker
❏ masking tape

For each pair of students:

❏ 1 envelope
❏ 1 copy of the two-sided Question Strips student sheet (masters on pages 114–115)
❏ 1 copy each of the Sorting Questions 1 and Sorting Questions 2 student sheets (masters on pages 112–113)
❏ the Scientific Journal (masters at back of guide) or 1 copy each of the Planning Our Investigation and Systematic Observation or Experiment? student sheets (masters on pages 108–111 and 116)

For each student:

❏ a pencil

Getting Ready

Before the Day of the Activity

1. Make one overhead transparency each of Planning Our Investigation (first page only; master on page 108), Sorting Questions 1 (master on page 112), Sorting Questions 2 (master on page 113), and Question Strips (front side only; master on page 114).

2. Cut the Question Strips transparency into nine individual strips so the questions can be sorted on the overhead.

3. Duplicate student sheets as necessary (masters on pages 108–116).

4. Cut one set of two-sided Question Strips and put them in an envelope for each pair of students.

5. Become familiar with the Investigation Rubric (master on page 126). Your students will be using parts of it when preparing for and conducting their investigations. In Session 3 you will project an overhead of the Investigation Rubric for students to refer to as they conduct their investigations.

6. Write the definition of an investigable question on butcher paper for posting later in the session. An *investigable question* is something possible to investigate and answer through doing an experiment or a systematic observation.

On the Day of the Activity

1. Set up the overhead projector and place the overhead transparencies and overhead pen near by.

2. Have envelopes containing the Question Strips on hand along with both Sorting Questions sheets.

3. If you are using Scientific Journals, have them on hand or prepare to distribute the appropriate pages depending on how you are managing the journal.

Introducing the Session

1. Focus the class on the list of "Questions We Have About Dry Ice" that they have generated throughout the unit. Tell the class that during the next two sessions, they will be working in pairs to plan their own dry ice investigations to answer a question that interests them. Let students know that once planned, they will carry out their investigations and share what they learned with others.

2. Explain that they will begin today's session by thinking more about what kinds of questions are needed for successful investigations as well as what investigation path to follow. One of the most important things about a successful investigation is coming up with the right kind of question. Tell students that after they have had some practice in identifying and crafting good questions, they will then choose the question they'd like to investigate.

Questions We Have About Dry Ice

• What is it made of?
• Why doesn't it get wet?
• Does it occur in nature?
• How is it made?
• Why doesn't it freeze fruit punch?
• How much gas does a small piece of dry ice make?
• Will a chunk twice the size make twice as much?
• Why does some metal squeak when it touches dry ice?

Questions That Are Hard to Investigate

1. Tell them that the first step is to come up with a question that is *investigable*—able to be investigated. Explain that in order to be investigable, a question must be possible to investigate (by doing a systematic observation or an experiment) and answer in their situation. (In their case, the situation is the classroom; in the case of a scientist, it might be a laboratory and/or a field site.) Post the butcher paper with the definition of an investigable question.

2. Ask, "What might make a question hard to investigate?" As students offer some of these or other ideas, provide a concrete example to illustrate:

- Not having the right equipment available. (e.g., How much does an elephant weigh?)

- Something that is too dangerous or impossible to do. (e.g., What would happen if we drilled a tunnel from one side of the Earth to the other?)

- Something that is too big a question. (e.g., What causes earthquakes?)

3. Point out that while these are **great questions,** they are not appropriate to answer by doing a single classroom investigation. We can still wonder about these questions, but these will not be ones that would be appropriate to choose to investigate.

4. Explain that there are other things that make questions hard to investigate besides the limits of equipment, danger, situation, and size of question. These other things are less obvious and need some practice to recognize.

5. Tell them that you have a short activity for them to do which will help them get good at coming up with investigable questions. You will give each pair of students a collection of questions. Their job will be to sort the questions according to those that seem investigable and those that do not.

Investigable Question:

An investigable question is something possible to investigate and answer through doing an experiment or a systematic observation.

Some teachers may prefer not to use the rather complex word "investigable," and rephrase it to "questions that are able to be investigated" or some other phrase. Although it may be hard to pronounce, "investigable" is concise and communicates exactly what is meant.

Categorizing Questions as Investigable or Not

1. Distribute an envelope containing the Question Strips and a Sorting Questions 1 student sheet to each pair of students, and ask them to sort the questions into three piles: "Investigable," "Not Investigable," and "Not Sure." Note: Instruct students to turn the strips so the italic writing is face down and the non-italic writing is face up. Circulate among the students, listening to their dialogue, asking questions, and providing clarifying information to prompt further analysis and consideration.

2. Before students are finished, prepare the overhead by putting the Sorting Questions 1 transparency on it with the transparencies of the Question Strips like those the students were given to sort.

3. After most pairs have finished sorting the questions, get the attention of the class. Ask for a pair to share how they grouped the questions. Set up this grouping on the overhead. Ask for their thinking behind why they grouped the questions that way.

4. Ask for hands of those who grouped in the same exact way. Ask for a pair that categorized one or more of the questions differently to share what they did (rearrange your transparency questions accordingly) and why. Do this a few more times, making sure that there has been a chance to discuss why or why not each question is or is not investigable. Guide the process by asking pointed questions, such as, "Can you think of an investigation we could do that would result in the answer to this question?"

5. Ideally this process of reflection and discussion will lead to a convergence of agreement about how to sort the strips. Allowing students to express disagreement is fruitful as a way of getting to agreement. By probing for discrepancies in opinions, you can help students see the logic of the classification more clearly.

If you are able to get to the following "correct" categorization of questions with the whole group (see below), that's great. Stop the discussion and continue with the activity.

If the group is a long way from agreement and there is not the time and/or interest to sustain a large group discussion, say something like the following:

"Some of these categorizations are arguable. If we had longer to discuss each one of these questions, I am sure that we could arrive at agreement about how they should be categorized. Scientists would most likely categorize the questions in the following way (rearrange the strips to be this way):"

Investigable

How much gas will one small piece of dry ice make?

Which takes longer to disappear, dry ice in a container of liquid or dry ice exposed to air?

Which is heavier, carbon dioxide gas or air?

If food coloring is added to water, will the dry ice fog be the color of the food coloring?

Will dry ice squeak when metal is pressed against it?

Not Investigable

How is dry ice made?

Why is dry ice dry?

How is the visible vapor from dry ice formed?

Why does dry ice sublime?

Generalizing About Investigable Questions

1. Ask the students to organize the questions as they are on the overhead and then turn over each strip so that the italic writing is face up. Explain that this tells what kind of question is on the front of the strip. It will look like this:

Investigable

"Measuring" question

"Comparison" question

"Comparison" question

"What-happens-if" question

"What-happens-if" question

Not Investigable

"How" question

"Why" question

"How" question

"Why" question

As new technologies are developed and less expensive ways of investigating are discovered, scientists find that what were formerly "uninvestigable" questions become investigable.

2. Help students generalize about investigable questions by asking them:

- In general, would you say that **"measuring" questions** are investigable? [yes]

- In general, would you say that **"what-happens-if" questions** are investigable? [yes]

- In general, would you say that **"comparison" questions** are investigable? [yes]

- In general, would you say that **"how" questions** are investigable? [no]

- In general, would you say that **"why" questions** are investigable? [no]

3. Point out that these generalizations are very useful in helping determine whether a question is investigable or not.

4. Summarize by saying that when students come up with a question to investigate, you will be using these criteria to evaluate whether it is a good investigable question. Put the transparency of page one of Planning Our Investigation on the overhead and reveal #1, #2, and the first set of checking points.

Framing an Investigable Question

1. Continue to focus students on the transparency of page one of Planning Our Investigation. Tell your students that when they begin planning their investigations, they will first need to think of the general topic or situation they want to find out more about. For example, they might want to find out more about the gas from dry ice, or why metal on dry ice squeaks, or the effect of dry ice on some other substance.

2. After they decide what they're interested in finding out more about, they will need to think of an investigable question—a question that is possible to answer through an experiment or systematic observation. Point out that this is what scientists do. While students might be interested in finding out more about a bigger topic area, they need to choose smaller questions that are possible to investigate in the classroom. Let students know that scientists might spend many years investigating a series of questions. Finding the answers to all these smaller questions may

eventually enable them to find out the answers to the bigger "how" and "why" questions.

3. To give students some practice in coming up with their own investigable questions, ask student pairs to brainstorm some, referring to the class list of "Questions We Have About Dry Ice." Point out that some of the questions on the list might already be phrased in a way that would make them investigable, but probably most will take some revising and focusing to transform them into something that can be investigated.

4. After several minutes, gather the attention of the class. Ask one pair to suggest an investigable question. Write it on the board.

5. Ask the class to agree whether it fits the criteria for being investigable. Have them suggest ways to modify the question to make it more investigable, or if it is not salvageable, ask for a different question.

6. Use this same process to come up with a second investigable question. If there is time, ask for a third. Point out that students will be choosing just one question when they do this.

Note: It is important to emphasize that even though "how" and "why" questions are often too general or for some other reason are unable to be briefly investigated with available materials in the classroom setting, they are the questions that have driven the process of discovery we call science. In a way science is all about the "why." The process this guide suggests for helping students understand and focus on investigable questions is not meant to downplay wondering why—on the contrary! Nor do we mean to imply a rigid way of looking at investigation—sometimes a "how" question may be able to be answered through a systematic observation; a comparison does not always need to imply a controlled experiment. There are many valid "variations" of experimentation and investigation, and scientists often have to creatively adapt to new conditions, situations, and technologies. Still, before one "creatively adapts," it is wise to know the basics—which is what these activities seek to convey. In a larger sense, the process of scientific investigation can perhaps be seen as the placing together of a series of "investigable questions" to then in fact arrive at or make progress toward understanding a larger "how" or "why" question. You may want to share some of these ideas with your students near the end of the unit.

Choosing an Investigation Pathway

1. Tell the class that just as important as choosing a good investigable question is choosing what kind of investigation to plan. Remind them of the two kinds of investigations that they have done so far in this unit:

- A **systematic observation** when they attempted to answer the question of, "What happens when you put dry ice in soap solution?"

- An **experiment** when they attempted to answer the question of, "Does temperature affect how fast dry ice turns to a gas?"

2. Ask them to recall what a systematic observation is. [Setting up a situation according to a plan and then carefully observing it over time.] Ask them to recall what an experiment is. [Comparing two situations where all variables are the same but one.]

3. Show the Sorting Questions 2 transparency. Tell them that they are going to again sort the Question Strips, but this time in these three categories: "best answered with a Systematic Observation," "best answered with an Experiment," or "Not Sure."

4. Before they begin, categorize a couple of sample questions as a group so they understand what they are to do. Use two of the questions that they came up with if there is an example of one experiment and one systematic observation. If not, use the following questions:

- "Which makes more gas, dry ice in warm water or dry ice in cold water?" ["comparison" question: best answered with an experiment]

- "How long will one small piece of dry ice produce fog?" ["measurement" question: best answered with a systematic observation]

5. Distribute a Sorting Questions 2 student sheet to each pair of students. Have the class take just the five questions categorized as "investigable" and now sort them into the three categories.

6. Circulate among students as they work, reminding them of the definitions of systematic observation and experiment. Some students may point out that some questions

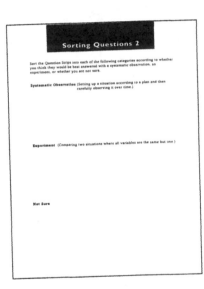

could be answered with either method; ask them to focus on how the question is phrased and whether or not it requires a comparison group.

7. Before the students are finished, prepare the overhead by adding the transparencies of the Question Strips to the Sorting Questions 2 transparency.

8. When most pairs are finished, regain their attention. Ask one pair to share how they categorized the questions. Arrange the Question Strips on the overhead accordingly. Probe for their thinking. Invite other pairs to suggest different ways to categorize the questions. Reemphasize that when a comparison is suggested, that would be best answered with an experiment.

9. If the class was able to agree on the following "correct" categorization of the questions, then stop the discussion and continue with the next part of the activity.

If the group is a long way from agreement or if they have agreed on something different, have them continue discussing, perhaps having them meet in small groups to come to agreement with each other before having a second round of discussion in the big group. If there is not the time and/or interest to sustain more discussion, you will again want to provide a respectful segue to the next step, by letting them know that the exact categorization is arguable, but with more time they would probably end up categorizing the questions in the way a scientist would (rearrange the strips to be this way):

Systematic Observation

How much gas will one small piece of dry ice make?

If food coloring is added to water, will the dry ice fog be the color of the food coloring?

Will dry ice squeak when metal is pressed against it?

Experiment

Which takes longer to disappear, dry ice in a container of liquid or dry ice exposed to air?

Which is heavier, carbon dioxide gas or air?

Generalizing About Appropriate Kinds of Investigations

1. Ask students to organize the Question Strips as they are on the overhead then turn them over and notice what kinds of questions are best answered by systematic observations and what kinds are best answered by experiments. It will look like this:

Systematic Observation

"Measuring" question

"What-happens-if" question

"What-happens-if" question

Experiment

"Comparison" question

"Comparison" question

2. Ask students to generalize about what kinds of questions are best answered by systematic observation. ["measuring" and "what-happens-if" questions] Ask what kinds of questions are best answered with experiments. ["comparison" questions]

3. Point out that many kinds of questions can be changed to become comparison questions. To demonstrate, single out the question "Will dry ice squeak when metal is pressed against it?" This "what-happens-if" question can be answered well by taking a metal key and pressing it against dry ice then observing what happens over time (a systematic observation). One could also turn it into a "comparison" question by rephrasing it, "Will different objects behave differently when they are pressed against dry ice?" Then one could compare what happens when a coin, a key, a pencil, and a plastic ruler are pressed against the dry ice. The investigation to answer the question becomes an experiment. Adding comparison groups is something that scientists often do and can broaden the focus of an investigation.

4. Summarize by saying that when students choose what investigation method to use, you will be using these criteria to evaluate whether it is appropriate. Put the transparency of page one of Planning Our Investigation back on the overhead and focus the group on the second set of checking points.

Some teachers make posters of the results of the question sorting and post them on the classroom wall. This provides a reminder of what types of questions are investigable and what investigation paths are best for each type of question.

Choosing Their Topic and an Investigable Question

Note: If you have time to do this next section now, it is worth doing it (or even just beginning it). Students have just been thinking about investigable questions and appropriate investigation pathways. If you don't have time in this session, it will fit nicely at the beginning of the next session, which is dedicated to planning. Either way can work.

1. Tell the class that it is now time for them to choose the general topic they are interested in investigating, to think of a good investigable question, and to decide whether they will conduct a systematic observation or an experiment.

2. You might want to tell the class that often people want to investigate something they think will have a "whiz bang" effect. For example, people often wonder what will happen if dry ice is mixed with acid (thinking it will have a huge and "cool" effect). They might choose a good investigable question and plan a great investigation that answers the question—but then feel disappointed when nothing much happens. Say that might be because what they were *really* wondering was, "Will something cool happen if I mix acid with dry ice?"

Explain that trying out things to see what makes a special effect was appropriate for the exploration phase—but now their purpose should be to answer a question they have about dry ice. They should consider their investigation a success if it answers their question—no matter what the result may be. They shouldn't expect that they will necessarily see dramatic effects nor should they just try things hoping to produce "whiz bang" results.

3. If they are not already organized into pairs, do that now. Ask them to designate one person as recorder and the other as checker. The job of the checker is to use the checking points to evaluate their work.

4. Have students turn to pages 11A–11D in their Scientific Journals, or distribute copies of the Planning Our Investigation student sheet to each pair of students and have them discuss and fill out the first page (what they are interested in finding out more about, what their investigable question will be, and whether they will design

Some teachers prefer to have each student keep their own recording sheets.

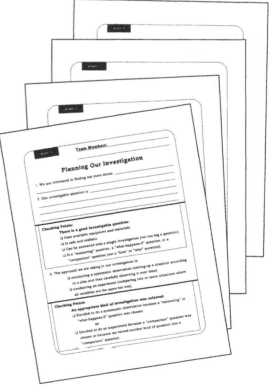

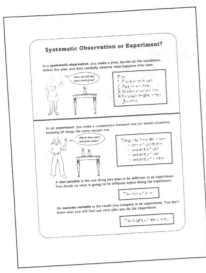

Some teachers have noticed that students need some additional motivation to create a rigorous investigation and evidence-based conclusions. While both scientists and students have the curiosity to drive an investigation, students usually haven't internalized the additional motivator—that science is the quest for truth, and the more rigorous they are in their investigations, the more likely they will come up with a finding that stands up to the scrutiny of other scientists (and becomes an accepted scientific fact, finding, or theory). Some teachers have chosen to challenge students to "Go out and prove something!" and have set up Session 4: Sharing Results of Investigations as a time when students "publish" and scrutinize each others' investigations. Other teachers have shared their reflections on rigor with students as they coach and advise them, especially when students are revising their investigations.

It is fine if different groups come up with similar questions; the important thing is that it interests them and that the question is a good, investigable question. You may want to point out that different groups of scientists often investigate similar questions and it has even happened that scientists in different places make the same discovery at about the same time—unbeknownst to each other!

a systematic observation or an experiment). As pairs choose their questions, ask students to turn to page 12 of their Scientific Journals or distribute copies of the Systematic Observation or Experiment? student sheet to remind them of the definitions of these two investigations.

5. Circulate, providing guidance as necessary. Students may have difficulty determining what kind of question they have proposed. When appropriate, encourage students to add a comparison group.

6. As table groups finish, have pairs trade questions with each other and use the checking points to critique each other's work.

7. Conclude by saying that in the next session, they will have a chance to design their own investigation plan.

Here is a very clear description of how science works, by the scientist who, in 1996, headed the team that detected possible evidence of life in an Antarctica meteor thought to be from Mars. You may want to share this with your students.

"Well, I must tell you about science and my feelings about it. I don't trust any scientific account all by itself. If it's really important but the work has been done only by one group—like ours—then I'm sorry, I wouldn't recommend it. What you want—just like a second opinion from a doctor—you want other experts to look too, because what I've learned from the years I've spent in science is that science is great at disproving things, but it's very poor at proving anything. It seems that if science can truly prove anything, it only does so by exhaustion—by having other people, other experts, repeat the research or the scientific test, and then if they can't think of any other explanation that makes sense out of what the first group of experts has claimed, there's a good chance that the results are correct. So although I'm bold enough to tell you that it is our best understanding and belief that the evidence today says there was primitive life on Mars, I'm prepared to change my mind if somebody brings me new evidence that brings me to a better interpretation of what we have seen."

—Dr. Richard Zare, Chairman of the National Science Board

Team Members: _____

_____

Planning Our Investigation

1. We are interested in finding out more about: _____

_____

2. Our investigable question is: _____

_____

_____

_____

Checking Points:

There is a good investigable question:

❏ Uses available equipment and materials.

❏ Is safe and realistic.

❏ Can be answered with a single investigation (*not* too big a question).

❏ Is a "measuring" question, a "what-happens-if" question, or a "comparison" question (*not* a "how" or "why" question).

3. The approach we are taking in our investigation is:

❏ conducting a systematic observation (setting up a situation according to a plan and then carefully observing it over time)

❏ conducting an experiment (comparing two or more situations where all variables are the same but one)

Checking Points:

An appropriate kind of investigation was selected:

❏ Decided to do a systematic observation because a "measuring" or "what-happens-if" question was chosen.

or

❏ Decided to do an experiment because a "comparison" question was chosen or because we turned another kind of question into a "comparison" question.

© 1999 by The Regents of the University of California, LHS-GEMS. *Dry Ice Investigations.* May be duplicated for classroom use.

© 1999 by The Regents of the University of California. LHS-GEMS. *Dry Ice Investigations.* **May be duplicated for classroom use.**

page 2

If you are conducting a **systematic observation**, please think through the following questions:

Things to decide (planning the conditions in the situation): _____

_____

_____

_____

_____

_____

Possible results (outcome variables): _____

_____

_____

_____

_____

Say if (and how) you plan to quantify the outcome: _____

_____

_____

_____

_____

If you are conducting an **experiment**, please think through the following questions:

Things to be changed (test variable): _____

_____

_____

_____

Things to stay the same (controlled variables): _____

_____

_____

_____

Result to be looked at (outcome variable): _____

_____

_____

_____

Say if (and how) you plan to quantify the outcome: _____

_____

_____

_____

© 1999 by The Regents of the University of California, LHS-GEMS. *Dry Ice Investigations*. **May be duplicated for classroom use.**

© 1999 by The Regents of the University of California, LHS-GEMS. *Dry Ice Investigations*. **May be duplicated for classroom use.**

page 4

Describe a plan for your systematic observation/experiment that takes all of these conditions and variables into account (use words and drawings):

Checking Points:

The investigation is well designed:

For Systematic Observations:

❏ Planned the conditions (variables).

❏ Identified possible outcome variables.

❏ Have clear and careful procedure that takes variables into account.

For Experiments:

❏ Identified test variable.

❏ Controlled variables.

❏ Identified outcome variable.

❏ Have clear and careful procedure that takes variables into account.

Sort the Question Strips into each of the following categories according to whether you think they are investigable, not investigable, or whether you are not sure.

Investigable (Can be answered by something you can *do* in the classroom—a systematic observation or an experiment.)

Not Investigable (Can **not** be answered by something you do firsthand in the classroom.)

Not Sure

© 1999 by The Regents of the University of California, LHS-GEMS. *Dry Ice Investigations*. **May be duplicated for classroom use.**

Sorting Questions 2

Sort the Question Strips into each of the following categories according to whether you think they would be best answered with a systematic observation, an experiment, or whether you are not sure.

Systematic Observation (Setting up a situation according to a plan and then carefully observing it over time.)

Experiment (Comparing two situations where all variables are the same but one.)

Not Sure

© 1999 by The Regents of the University of California, LHS-GEMS. *Dry Ice Investigations.* **May be duplicated for classroom use.**

How is dry ice made?

Why is dry ice dry?

How is the visible vapor from dry ice formed?

Why does dry ice sublime?

How much gas will one small piece of dry ice make?

Which takes longer to disappear, dry ice in a container of liquid or dry ice exposed to air?

Which is heavier, carbon dioxide gas or air?

If food coloring is added to water, will the dry ice fog be the color of the food coloring?

Will dry ice squeak when metal is pressed against it?

© 1999 by The Regents of the University of California. LHS-GEMS. Dry Ice Investigations. May be duplicated for classroom use.

"How" question

"Why" question

"How" question

"Why" question

"Measuring" question

"Comparison" question

"Comparison" question

"What-happens-if" question

"What-happens-if" question

© 1999 by The Regents of the University of California, LHS-GEMS. *Dry Ice Investigations*. **May be duplicated for classroom use.**

Systematic Observation or Experiment?

In a *systematic observation*, you make a plan, decide on the conditions, follow the plan, and then carefully observe what happens over time.

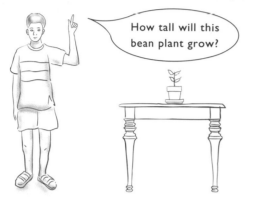

How tall will this bean plant grow?

Plan:
1. Plant bean in soil.
2. Put near window.
3. Water once per day.
4. Measure height after 3 weeks.

In an *experiment*, you make a comparison between two (or more) situations, keeping all things the same except one.

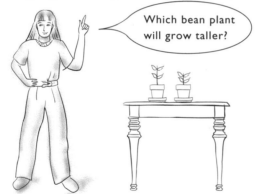

Which bean plant will grow taller?

Things to keep the same:
• size of container
• amount of soil
• amount of sun
• amount of water

A *test variable* is the one thing you plan to be different in an experiment. You decide on what is going to be different *before* doing the experiment.

The kind of bean

An *outcome variable* is the result you compare in an experiment. You don't know what you will find out until *after* you do the experiment.

The height of the plants

© 1999 by The Regents of the University of California, LHS-GEMS. Dry Ice Investigations. **May be duplicated for classroom use.**

Session 2: Making an Investigation Plan

Planning something is often not as fun or compelling as doing the thing itself. But failure to plan almost always results in a lower quality experience. This is certainly true for planning scientific investigations! Depending on their age and experience, your students will need more or less time and guidance to plan their investigations. You can choose to provide the opportunity and guidance for planning in several ways:

1) You can give the class an entire session to plan on their own, completing their Planning Our Investigation sheets, then beginning their Our Dry Ice Investigation sheets, and determining what materials they will need. During the session you can move from group to group giving them advice, answering questions, and clarifying terms. (Step-by-step instructions for this type of planning process are included in the pages that follow.)

2) You can have students do their planning entirely on their own as homework, over several different evenings. You may want to review their individual plans before allowing them to proceed.

3) You can let students explore with dry ice one more time in order to refine their questions, devise ways to control variables, and choose a way to measure the outcome variable.

Different planning methods will be better for different groups of students. The instructions that follow relate to method #1.

As in the previous planning session, students are given checking points to use in honing and evaluating their investigation plans.

Some teachers have chosen to provide more practice planning experiences. Small groups plan a systematic observation and an experiment involving something other than dry ice. For example, students plan a systematic observation designed to answer the question, "How big a (gum) bubble can we blow?" They also plan an experiment to answer the question, "Which blows bigger bubbles, regular bubble gum or sugarless bubble gum?" In each case, students determine the conditions of the investigation, the possible effects (outcome variables), if and how they plan to quantify the outcome, and (in the case of the experiment) the thing to be changed (test variable) and the things that stay the same (controlled variables). Then as an entire class, the planning is critiqued. Depending on the experience of your class and their ability to transfer lessons gained from the bubble gum (or other) example to their dry ice investigation, this can be a very useful student learning experience.

What You Need

For each student:
- ❏ the Scientific Journal (masters at back of guide) or 1 copy each of the Our Dry Ice Investigation and Materials List student sheets (masters on pages 120–122), and the Planning Our Investigation student sheet (from last session)
- ❏ a pencil

Getting Ready

Before the Day of the Activity

Duplicate student sheets as necessary (masters on pages 120–122).

On the Day of the Activity

If you are using Scientific Journals, have them on hand or prepare to distribute the appropriate pages depending on how you are managing the journal.

Planning their Investigations

1. Remind the class that in the last session, they chose an investigable question and the best investigation path for answering that question: either a systematic observation or an experiment (the first page of the Planning Our Investigation student sheet).

2. Tell them that in this session, they will complete their planning for their investigation (the remaining pages of the Planning Our Investigation sheet). You may want to give the example that planning a trip is not nearly as fun as going on a trip, but that unplanned trips can be disasters. The same is true for investigations. Today, through planning, they will ensure that their investigation will be a good one.

3. Let students know that they are to complete pages 11B and 11D of Planning Our Investigation (if they are doing a systematic observation) or pages 11C and 11D (if they are doing an experiment). On page 11D they will actually describe their plan, taking into account all of the thinking they do about the variables in their investigation. Encourage them to discuss a number of ideas for methods before they decide on one.

4. Point out that at the bottom of page 11D there are more checking points for them to use, to ensure they have planned a carefully thought through investigation. Suggest that they look at those checking points first. (Have the partner that did not serve as the checker in the last session, serve as a checker today. The other partner can be the recorder.)

5. Tell them that you will also be distributing Materials List student sheets for them to complete, indicating those materials that they will need that they know are in the classroom, and those that they will need some help locating. *Note:* You may want to involve students in getting the materials together. If so, decide how you want to do this and mention it here.

6. When the students understand what they are to do, either distribute the Planning Our Investigation student sheet or instruct students to turn to pages 11A–11D in their Scientific Journals. Distribute the Materials List student sheet.

7. Circulate among the students, providing guidance, encouragement, and good input as needed. Remind them to complete their Materials List.

8. As groups finish, ask students to turn to page 13A of their Scientific Journal or distribute and have students complete the first page of the Our Dry Ice Investigation sheet in preparation for the next session. Collect the Materials List sheets from students.

Note: You may want to provide feedback to each group on their investigation plan before they proceed. If so, decide on your method for doing this and mention it to students now.

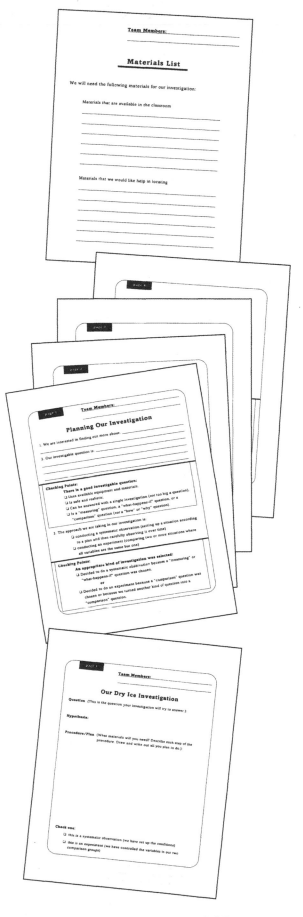

Team Members: _____

_____

Materials List

We will need the following materials for our investigation:

Materials that are available in the classroom

_____

_____

_____

_____

_____

_____

Materials that we would like help in locating

_____

_____

_____

_____

_____

_____

© 1999 by The Regents of the University of California, LHS-GEMS. *Dry Ice Investigations.* **May be duplicated for classroom use.**

© 1999 by The Regents of the University of California, LHS-GEMS. *Dry Ice Investigations.* **May be duplicated for classroom use.**

Team Members: _____

_____

Our Dry Ice Investigation

Question (This is the question your investigation will try to answer.):

Hypothesis:

Procedure/Plan (What materials will you need? Describe each step of the procedure. Draw and write out all you plan to do.):

Check one:

❏ this is a systematic observation (we have set up the conditions)

❏ this is an experiment (we have controlled the variables in our two comparison groups)

page 2

Our Dry Ice Investigation (continued)

Results (What happened? What did you observe? Be very clear and precise. If you quantified the outcome, share that information here.):

Conclusion (What do the results tell you? Were the results the same as your hypothesis or not?):

Explanation (How can you explain the results?):

Problems (Were there any problems? What might you do differently if you did the test again?):

More Questions (Did the test make you think of more questions?):

© 1999 by The Regents of the University of California, LHS-GEMS. Dry Ice Investigations. May be duplicated for classroom use.

Session 3: Conducting Investigations

In this session, students conduct their carefully planned investigations. Early finishers are encouraged to conduct follow-up investigations to answer new questions that arise. Again, students have access to the checking points that will be used to evaluate their investigation reports and the scientific reasoning that they use.

What You Need

For the class:

- ❏ dry ice (about 1 slab)
- ❏ hammer
- ❏ 2 cloths (old T-shirts or T-shirt sized rags)
- ❏ small insulated container for storing pieces of dry ice
- ❏ other materials as indicated by student groups (See "Getting Ready" 3 below.)
- ❏ 16 trays
- ❏ an overhead transparency of the Investigation Rubric (master on page 126)
- ❏ overhead projector
- ❏ extension cord (if needed for overhead projector)

For each student:

- ❏ the Scientific Journal (masters at back of guide) or 1 copy of the Follow-Up Investigation student sheet (master on page 127) and the Our Dry Ice Investigation student sheet (from last session)
- ❏ a pencil

Getting Ready

Before the Day of the Activity

1. Plan how you will get dry ice. (See the section entitled "Obtaining and Maintaining Dry Ice" on page 7.) This session requires about one slab of dry ice for a class of 32 students.

2. Make an overhead transparency of the Investigation Rubric (master on page 126).

3. Review the Materials Lists that your students prepared in the last session. If necessary, get a couple of students to consolidate the lists into one for you.

4. Acquire the remaining materials needed for this session.

5. Duplicate student sheets as necessary (masters on pages 126–127).

On the Day of the Activity

1. In a central location, place the materials that students have indicated they will need.

2. Set out a stack of trays so pairs of students can easily transport the materials they will need.

3. Set up the overhead projector and place the overhead transparency near by.

4. If you are using Scientific Journals, have them on hand or prepare to distribute the appropriate pages depending on how you are managing the journal.

Immediately Before Class

Lay a slab of dry ice on a towel, T-shirt, or other rag. Place another towel or cloth on top of it. Use the side of a hammer to break the dry ice through the rag. Put the broken pieces in a small insulated container.

Conducting Investigations

1. Tell the class they will now get to carry out the investigations they have planned! Distribute the Our Dry Ice Investigation student sheets or instruct students to turn to

pages 13A and 13B in their Scientific Journals. If they haven't done so already, they will need to complete the first page of the Our Dry Ice Investigation student sheet (Question, Hypothesis, and Procedure/Plan) before they begin.

2. Tell students where the materials are located, and explain any rules they must follow in getting them.

3. Remind the students to fill out the second page of the Our Dry Ice Investigation student sheet (Results, Conclusion, Explanation, Problems, and More Questions) during and after they have performed their investigation. It is fine to illustrate their results as well as describe what happens in words.

4. Put the transparency of the Investigation Rubric on the overhead and tell students that they should use the following standards to guide their work. These are the evaluation criteria that you will be using for this second page of their investigation report.

5. Tell students if they finish at least 15 minutes before the end of the session, and want to refine and repeat their experiment, they can do so. They can also conduct an additional investigation to answer a question that arose. If they want to do either of these things, they should come to you and ask for a Follow-Up Investigation student sheet or turn to page 14 in their Scientific Journals.

6. When the students understand what they are to do, have them get the materials they need, and begin their investigations. Monitor the distribution of dry ice (as needed) and make sure all pairs are proceeding in a cooperative fashion. Encourage students to carefully record what they are observing and discovering.

7. If some teams finish early, allow them to begin planning other tests they would like to do to answer questions of their choice. Depending on time constraints, some students may be able to do one or more follow-up investigations. If they do, make sure they fill out a Follow-Up Investigation sheet for each one.

8. When the teams have finished, have them take all the materials to a central location, following your clean up instructions.

Investigation Rubric

1) There is a good investigable question:

- ❏ Uses available equipment and materials.
- ❏ Is safe and realistic.
- ❏ Can be answered with a single investigation (not too big a question).
- ❏ Is a "measuring" question, a "what-happens-if" question, or a "comparison" question (not a "how" or "why" question).

2) An appropriate kind of investigation was selected:

- ❏ Decided to do a systematic observation because a "measuring" or "what happens-if" question was chosen.

    or

- ❏ Decided to do an experiment because a "comparison" question was chosen or because we turned another kind of question into a "comparison" question.

3) The investigation is well designed:

For Systematic Observations:
- ❏ Planned the conditions (variables).
- ❏ Identified possible outcome variables.
- ❏ Have clear and careful procedure that takes variables into account.

For Experiments:
- ❏ Identified test variable.
- ❏ Controlled variables.
- ❏ Identified outcome variable.
- ❏ Have clear and careful procedure that takes variables into account.

4) Careful reasoning is used:

- ❏ Used data and results to support conclusions.
- ❏ Suggested a well-reasoned explanation.
- ❏ Thought through problems and additional questions.

5) Ideas are well-communicated:

- ❏ Ideas are clearly expressed through writing and diagrams so others can understand your investigation and your reasoning.

© 1999 by The Regents of the University of California, LHS-GEMS. *Dry Ice Investigations.* **May be duplicated for classroom use.**

Follow-Up Investigation

Our first Investigation Question was:

The follow-up question we want to investigate is:

Hypothesis:

Procedure/Plan (Describe each step of the procedure. Draw and write out all you plan to do.):

Results (What happened? What did you observe? Be very clear and precise. If you quantified the outcome, share that information here.):

Conclusion (What do the results tell you? Were the results the same as your hypothesis or not?):

Explanation (How can you explain the results?):

© 1999 by The Regents of the University of California, LHS-GEMS. *Dry Ice Investigations*. **May be duplicated for classroom use.**

Session 4: Sharing Results of Investigations

In this session, students share the results of their dry ice investigations. Providing students with an opportunity to share what they discovered is important. Finding a way to do this that is not boring or interminable is the challenge; and is different for every situation. Thus, a number of options are suggested to provide you with ideas for this important closure to your students' investigation experience.

Getting Ready

1. Choose how you want to structure this session.

2. Acquire any materials that are needed.

Poster Session
This is a forum that scientists often use to share the results of their work. Have student groups set up their investigation reports on posters around the room (they can be set up at their work tables). One partner can stand next to the poster and answer questions as other students come by while the other partner can check out other group's experiments. Then they can switch.

Sentence Strip Bonanza
Each investigation group can meet to discuss the following four points: what they discovered, what was most surprising, the biggest problem they had, the most burning question they have now. Groups record these four things on sentence strips and post the sentence strips by category (discoveries, surprises, problems, burning new questions). The teacher then leads a facilitated discussion of each category, shortening the discussion when attention wanes.

Peer Review
Each group reviews another group's investigation, using the investigation rubric, and writes a note back with what was strong and what could use improvement. Students have the opportunity to revise their reports before turning them in to the teacher for evaluation.

Publishing Their Results

Assign your students to write dry ice "news articles," including information from their investigations. You can then do a bulletin board newspaper layout ("The Dry Ice Gas-zette") incorporating student articles or actually "publish" the newspaper and share with parents.

Oral Reports

Students can orally report what they did and field questions from the class. Groups that did similar investigations can be scheduled one after another; each group can add to what the group before did by saying what they did that was similar; what they discovered that was different; or what questions arose for them.

Extra Credit: Some teachers offer students extra credit for explaining what might be happening at the molecular level in their investigation.

Going Further *(for the entire unit)*

Make a Dry Ice Comet
Dry ice can be used to simulate comets and teach students about them. There are several "recipes" for dry ice comets available on the Internet. Here are three web sites that provide step-by-step instructions:

- Let's Cook Up a Comet
  by Dennis Schatz of the Pacific Science Center
  http://news3.news.wisc.edu/011cometscrecipe.html
- How to Make a Comet
  in the Backyard Science Center of the Internet Space Station on the International Space Physics Educational Consortium's site
  http://ispec.ucsd.edu/station/backyard/
  make_a_comet.html
- Making a Comet in the Classroom
  from Dennis Schatz with an introduction by NASA
  http://lunar.ksc.nasa.gov/education/spaceday/activity/
  making_T.html

To find more recipes for making comets, do an Internet search using the key words "dry ice" and "comet."

Michael Jordans of the Mind
Have students do research on scientists who have had a large influence in changing the direction of science or whose scientific skills and new ways of looking at things made new breakthroughs in science. Some possible names include: Copernicus, Galileo, Lavoisier, Marie Curie, Albert Einstein, George Washington Carver, Charles Drew, Barbara McClintock, and Glenn Seaborg.

Dry Ice Riddles
Have your students write riddles about dry ice. You may want to require them to contain a designated minimum number of properties and/or facts of dry ice. For example, "What blows bubbles, is in many rock concerts, is colder than winter, is white as snow, and doesn't like to get wet?"

Science Fair Projects
If your school is having a science fair, you may want to encourage your students to present an investigation they performed, do one they didn't have time to do in class, or make a more extensive investigation of dry ice and related topics.

In Search of CO$_2$

Students try to find gases in their lives and test them to see if they're CO$_2$. They test them using a test for CO$_2$ (bubbling it through lime water to make CaCO$_3$ precipitate) or an acid indicator. Testing could include: yeast, baking soda and vinegar, breath, soda gas, elodea, fire extinguishers, fizzies, alka-seltzer, bicycle pump, car exhaust, styrofoam (or cornstarch) air pockets, pockets in bread, etc.

Candle in a Jar

Students observe an experiment in which a jar is placed upside down over a burning candle in a dish of colored water. The candle extinguishes, and the liquid rises inside the jar. The explanation is complicated, but it's a great opportunity for students to try to come up with their own explanations.

Alka-Seltzer

Students examine the different fizzing of alka-seltzer in hot and cold water. A number of other experiments, including emphasis on controls, can be done with alka-seltzer.

Fire Extinguisher

Students make fire extinguishers by constructing something that keeps the baking soda and vinegar separate until shaken, when it squirts CO$_2$ out of a plastic tube.

Elodea in BTB

Students blow into BTB (bromothymol blue—an indicator) and observe how it turns green with CO$_2$ gas. Students put elodea (an aquatic plant) in, and observe how the BTB turns blue with oxygen.

Cloud Chamber/Subatomic Particles

Put dry ice on top of a sealed container with alcohol inside. The alcohol will form a gas. You can watch the trails from subatomic particles. A magnet can be used to direct them.

Behind the Scenes

The scientific subject matter connected to dry ice, like the gas that dry ice transforms into, expands outward in many directions! Chemistry texts and reference books can provide more complete background than this necessarily limited discussion. In this section, we provide some basic information concerning dry ice and carbon dioxide (CO_2), phases and phase change, and the particulate theory of matter. Separate background information is also provided on student misconceptions concerning these topics as well as on the development of inquiry abilities and understandings in students.

In *Dry Ice Investigations*, students place pieces of dry ice in plastic cups and observe what happens. The dry ice "sublimes." How do we know that dry ice actually changes into carbon dioxide gas? Like air, and all matter, carbon dioxide gas occupies volume. If you put a few small pieces of dry ice in a plastic bag, squeeze the air out, and seal the bag, you can catch the carbon dioxide gas as the dry ice disappears. Carbon dioxide gas has different chemical properties from air. It does not support combustion or respiration. A glowing wooden splint carefully inserted into the bag of carbon dioxide will go out. See the table on page 136 for other ways that carbon dioxide is unique.

Experiments, such as those your students conduct in this unit, sometimes allow us to gather information about things that are too small to see. You can plainly see the piece of dry ice sitting in the plastic cup. But even the most powerful magnifying glass will not show you that it is made of billions of billions of vibrating carbon dioxide molecules packed together—or that each carbon dioxide molecule is two oxygen atoms connected to one carbon atom in a linear arrangement—or that the arrangement and movement of molecules in a solid is different from that of molecules in a liquid or a gas. By grappling with the behavior of dry ice, this unit helps introduce students to the particulate model of matter as the best current scientific explanation for the nature and behavior of matter.

The following information is provided to the teacher to assist you in responding to student questions. That's why we have written it in a question-driven format. **It is not intended to be read out loud to students or duplicated for them to read.** GEMS guides are revised frequently, and we welcome your suggestions!

Dry Ice and Carbon Dioxide

What is dry ice?

Dry ice is frozen carbon dioxide. When carbon dioxide gas is lowered to −78.4°C (−109°F) it takes on a solid form.

How cold is dry ice?

Dry ice is very cold. A sample of solid carbon dioxide remains at its sublimation point, −78.4°C, (−109°F) until it is all gone.

Can dry ice burn you?

If you touch dry ice for more than just an instant, your skin and tissues can freeze to death. This really hurts! It feels like a severe burn.

How was dry ice discovered?

The first person to prepare solid carbon dioxide was a French chemist, Thirolier, who experimented with liquefied gases. He engineered better ways of compressing gases, and introduced the use of strong metal cylinders to contain them. Using the metal cylinders, Thirolier could work with higher pressures than his other contemporaries, who used glass. But because he could not see inside his cylinders, he had to open the metal cylinder to observe a liquid he had prepared. This only gave him a short time to observe the liquid before it evaporated. Other scientists had noticed that evaporation lowered the temperature of the remaining liquid sample, which made it last longer for them to observe. They understood that as the liquid evaporated to gas, heat was taken from the liquid, making it much cooler. (This discovery probably happened by accident; the glass containers they used to keep liquefied gases in often broke!) One day in 1835, Thirolier prepared a large sample of liquid carbon dioxide. When he opened his cylinder, the temperature drop due to evaporation was so large that the remaining liquid in the cylinder froze solid!

How is dry ice made?

Instead of using fancy refrigerators to cool carbon dioxide gas all the way down to −78°C, manufacturers of dry ice take advantage of the phase changes of carbon dioxide in part of the refrigeration process. The process starts with a tank of liquid carbon dioxide at 63 atmospheres (atm) pressure. The carbon dioxide is sent through a small nozzle into a tower at lower pressure. The pressure change causes the liquid to change into gas. As a liquid evaporates to gas, heat is released. Heat energy leaves the liquid carbon dioxide as it evaporates. As more and more evaporates, the temperature of the liquid and the evaporating gas gets lower and lower. Expanding into a space at lower pressure also causes most gases (except for hydrogen and helium) to cool. In the case of carbon dioxide, the expanding gas cools so much that about half of it turns into "snow flakes" of solid carbon dioxide. The flakes are then mechanically pressed into blocks or pellets. You can make your own carbon dioxide dry ice "snow" by discharging a carbon dioxide fire extinguisher. The carbon dioxide in an extinguisher is under 63 atm of pressure. When you press on the release valve, the carbon dioxide shoots out into the air, where there is much less pressure (1 atmosphere). When fired, you can see small particles of dry ice snow mentioned above.

The invention of the fire extinguisher is attributed to an African-American scientist, T.J. Marshall, in 1872.

What is dry ice used for?

Dry ice has many uses. Both dry ice and liquid carbon dioxide are used as refrigerants in the food industry, and have been recognized as safe for these purposes for many years. Among food applications are: frozen food storage and transportation; meat packing and processing; airline catering; and carbonation of beverages. Dry ice and/or liquid carbon dioxide are also used by dermatologists, blood banks, in various chemical processes, for control of pH, in pharmaceutical manufacturing, and in many other situations requiring cooling or refrigeration. Another interesting and relatively recent application is cryogenic blasting—an alternative to other cleaning methods, such as sandblasting and cleaning with solvents. Dry ice blast cleaning is used in food processing, for molded products, and in automotive, aerospace, general maintenance, and many other industries. It is considered environmentally more friendly than cleaning processes that require secondary cleanup of their wastes, and it permits the cleaning of equipment "in place" thus reducing labor costs and down time. In addition to its use as a dry cleaning solvent, liquid carbon dioxide is also used as an agent for extracting oil from shale, as a medium for the disposal of hazardous waste, and to extract caffeine from coffee. Dry ice has also been used to "seed" clouds to cause rainfall on a small scale.

What causes fog from dry ice?

Solid carbon dioxide normally sublimes to gaseous form at −78°C or warmer. This means that the gas coming off the dry ice is very cold at first. When this cold gas encounters air, water vapor in the air condenses into a fog. This fog is made of the same stuff as the fog you'd find by a river in the early morning— tiny droplets of liquid water. But the amount of cold gas from the dry ice is very small compared to the amount of warm air and other warm objects in the room. Soon, everything warms up to room temperature. At room temperature, the fog disappears as the liquid water droplets change back into water vapor. **It is important for you and your students to recognize that the "fog" coming off the dry ice is *not* carbon dioxide gas itself but condensation of the water vapor in the air. The fog is a sign that the cold gas is present, but is not the gas itself!**

What are the properties of carbon dioxide?

In this unit, carbon dioxide is observed both as a solid and as a gas. Solid carbon dioxide is often called "dry ice" because it looks like solid water and doesn't turn to liquid. Carbon dioxide gas was once called "fixed air" because it is colorless and odorless like ordinary air. How can we determine whether a substance is really carbon dioxide? The following table summarizes the main chemical and physical properties of carbon dioxide as compared to water and air, as one way to show the properties that make carbon dioxide unique.

Comparison of Carbon Dioxide to Water and Air (Nitrogen and Oxygen)

	Carbon Dioxide	Water	Air (Mixture of Nitrogen and Oxygen)	
	CO_2	H_2O	N_2	O_2
solid Color of liquid gas	white colorless * colorless	white colorless colorless	white colorless colorless	
Odor	odorless	odorless	odorless	
Molecular Mass	44 amu	18 amu	28 amu	32 amu
Density at room temperature	1.931 g/L	997.0 g/L	1.161 g/L	
Normal state at room temperature	gas	liquid	gas	
Normal phase changes	sublimes at −78.4°C	melts at 0.0°C boils at 100.0°C	melts at −213.4°C boils at −194.5°C	
Solubility in water	0.034 M/atm Solution is acidic	—	0.00067 M/atm Neutral	0.0012 M/atm Neutral
Role in respiration and combustion	Produced	Produced	Not involved	Needed
Role in photosynthesis	Needed	Needed	Not involved	Produced
Reactions with minerals	CO_2 slowly reacts with metal oxides to form carbonates.	Some minerals are slightly soluble in water.	N_2 does not react with minerals.	O_2 slowly reacts with elemental metals to form metal oxides.
Reactions with acids	Carbonates react vigorously with acids to form solutions and CO_2 bubbles.			Metal oxides react with acids to form solutions.
Planetary atmospheres	Venus 96.4 % Earth 0.03 % Mars 95.32 %	Venus 0.1 % Earth 0–3 % Mars 0.03 %	Venus 3.4 % Earth 78.08 % Mars 2.7 %	Venus 0.0069 % Earth 20.95 % Mars 0.13 %

* Liquid CO_2 is not observed at atmospheric pressure, but can be produced at higher pressures.

Where is carbon dioxide found?
Does dry ice occur naturally anywhere?

You are probably already familiar with many roles of carbon dioxide in the environment.

CO_2 and Breathing. When you breathe in air, your blood carries the oxygen from the air into your body tissues. There, it undergoes a series of carefully controlled reactions with glucose, which is stored food. Overall, the oxygen reacts with the glucose to produce energy, carbon dioxide gas, and liquid water. Your blood carries the carbon dioxide back to your lungs and you breathe it out. Carbon dioxide gas does not support respiration—if a person were trapped in a room filled with carbon dioxide without any oxygen, they would die.

CO_2 and Burning. When you burn an organic fuel, such as wood or gasoline, a similar, but much faster, process occurs. In the overall reaction, oxygen reacts with fuel to produce energy, carbon dioxide gas, and water. Carbon dioxide does not support combustion—you can extinguish a fire by spraying it with carbon dioxide, which is why many fire extinguishers are filled with it.

CO_2 and Photosynthesis. Green plants need carbon dioxide to grow. They use photosynthesis to obtain the opposite results of human respiration. In this process, energy from sunlight is used to make carbon dioxide gas react with water. Glucose (food) and oxygen gas are produced.

CO_2 and Minerals. Carbon dioxide in the air slowly reacts with certain rocks in the Earth's crust to form carbonate-containing minerals. Calcium carbonate ($CaCO_3$) is one very common example; some of the many forms of calcium carbonate are limestone, marble, and chalk. Seashells are also mostly calcium carbonate. Another well-known carbonate is baking soda, sodium hydrogen carbonate ($NaHCO_3$). When these carbonate-containing minerals come in contact with acids, bubbles of carbon dioxide return to the air. Familiar examples are the reaction between baking soda and vinegar (acetic acid), and the reaction between marble statues and acid rain.

CO_2 and Planetary Atmospheres. Carbon dioxide gas is found in the atmospheres of Venus, Earth, and Mars. Only a small fraction of the Earth's atmosphere is carbon dioxide; even though carbon dioxide is continually added to the atmosphere by animal respiration and combustion, it is continually being removed by photosynthesizing green plants. There is no known life on Venus or Mars, and carbon dioxide is the major component of those atmospheres. On Mars, it is so cold that some of the carbon dioxide deposits as solid dry ice on the polar ice caps.

What gases are in Earth's air?
78% nitrogen
21% oxygen
0.9% argon
0.03% carbon dioxide
0.07% other gases, such as neon, krypton and xenon

The amount of carbon dioxide in the air is estimated to have increased by 25% since 1880! For more information on the impact of carbon dioxide on global temperature, see the activities and background information in the GEMS unit Global Warming and the Greenhouse Effect.

Why does dry ice sublimate?

Dry ice sublimates because—under the conditions of temperature and pressure found, for example, in your students' experimental cup—carbon dioxide's unique and characteristic molecular structure and properties cause the solid form (which can only exist at $-78°C$ or below) to transform into the gaseous form. In this case, energy added to a solid turns it to a gas. At the Earth's usual atmospheric pressure (defined as 1 atm) as the solid form of dry ice becomes "warmer" than $-78°C$, the kinetic energy and movement of the molecules increases enough to escape all of the attractive forces that hold the solid together. Molecules move into whatever space is available. We are all familiar with the phase changes of water, which include ice (a solid), water (a liquid), and steam (a gas) depending on the heat energy involved. Carbon dioxide however can only exist in the liquid form when it is subjected to pressures above 5.1 atm. Therefore at room temperature and standard pressure it behaves in the surprising way your students witness—it changes from a solid to a gas—or sublimates. It is not the only substance that acts in this way, but it is surely one of the most exciting! (See the longer discussion of phases and phase change later in this background section and the Phase Change Diagram on page 144 for more information on this direct but complex question!)

What affects how fast a piece of dry ice sublimates?

Surface area is a primary factor. Sublimation occurs only at the surface of a piece of dry ice. So, it makes sense that the rate of sublimation is directly proportional to the surface area. If you increase the surface area by breaking a piece of dry ice into smaller bits, it will sublimate faster. Surface area is a key factor in many other physical processes. Liquids evaporate faster if they have more surface area. A puddle of water "disappears" from the floor faster than the same amount of water evaporates from a glass. Also, solids with more surface area dissolve faster. Powdered sugar dissolves in water faster than a hard lump of sugar.

Heating rate. Heat energy is required to convert a solid into a gas, and the rate of sublimation increases when you increase the heating rate. Heat flows into a cold piece of dry ice whenever it touches a warmer object. This warmer object could be anything in the room—a metal plate, a wooden table, liquid water, or even the air around the dry ice. Heat flows faster when there is a greater temperature difference between the warm object and the cold dry ice. For example, dry ice sublimes faster when it touches a hot metal plate than when it touches a cool spoon or tongs.

Why does dry ice glide on a hot plate or on a table?

Pieces of dry ice glide on cushions of carbon dioxide gas, just as hovercraft glide on cushions of air. But unlike hovercraft, pieces of dry ice are entirely surrounded by their cushions of gas. Why do pieces of dry ice glide around on cushions of carbon dioxide gas? When a cold piece of dry ice touches any warm surface, the rate of sublimation increases at the point of contact. At atmospheric pressure (1 atm) the sublimed carbon dioxide gas would take up 2000 times as much space as it did in its solid form! But in the piece of dry ice, the gas is compressed into a much smaller volume. Very quickly,

You might be tempted to place a closed bag of dry ice on a balance, to show that mass is conserved when solid carbon dioxide changes into a gas. We don't recommend trying this experiment, because the actual results are very confusing. Of course the mass of carbon dioxide does not change, but the reading on the balance will go down! This is because there's air in the room. At the beginning of the experiment, the reading on the balance reflects the mass of the plastic bag, the carbon dioxide, and the air over the balance. At the end of the experiment, the reading on the balance reflects the mass of the plastic bag, the carbon dioxide, and less air — some has been pushed away as the carbon dioxide changed from solid to gas and made the bag bigger.

the pressure of carbon dioxide gas becomes high enough to overcome the force of gravity that pulls the piece of dry ice down. As the gas escapes from underneath, the solid can be lifted (just a tiny bit) away from the surface. The solid carbon dioxide continues to sublime, and the gas continues to escape from beneath it. The escaping gas acts as a cushion that greatly reduces friction between the dry ice and the surface. This leads to the gliding behavior—with less friction, a small push sends a piece of dry ice into a long glide. So why don't dry ice pieces really hover like hovercraft? There is a second important difference between the two. Most of the energy used for subliming the dry ice comes from the warm conductive surface, not the air. As the carbon dioxide gas begins to lift the solid away from the surface, the rate of sublimation slows down. Hovercraft do not share this slowing down process—they carry their air blowing equipment, which creates a constant cushion under the craft, with them wherever they go.

Why does dry ice sink when large, then float when small?

Objects sink if they weigh more than an equal volume of water, and float if they weigh less. Drop a large piece of dry ice into water, and it will sink to the bottom, bubbling furiously. Later, as it gets smaller, it will be buoyed up by the bubbles of carbon dioxide that cling to its surface, and it will float. Operating under very similar principles, submarines sink when their ballast tanks are filled with water and float when their ballast tanks are filled with air. A lump of solid carbon dioxide without any bubbles sinks because it weighs more than the water it displaces. A bubble of carbon dioxide gas floats because it weighs less than the water it displaces. A bubble of carbon dioxide *and* a piece of dry ice stuck together could sink or float, depending on the relative amounts of gas and solid. If the ratio of gas to solid is high enough, the dry-ice-and-bubbles will be light enough to float. Since the gas bubbles form at the surface of dry ice pieces, pieces of dry ice with large surface area to volume ratios can attain large gas to solid ratios and will float. For any regular solid shape, the surface area to volume ratio increases as the size of the solid decreases. Thus, large pieces of dry ice sink and the small ones float.

In the case of dry ice, the "object" that sinks or floats is actually the piece of solid carbon dioxide together with the bubbles of gas on its surface. (Even though it looks as if the bubbles are "clinging" to the surface of the solid, the surface tension of the surrounding water actually holds them there.)

Why do small pieces of dry ice "dance" around on the surface of water and bounce away from other objects?

Small pieces of dry ice float, for reasons described above. As the dry ice sublimes, it releases carbon dioxide gas from its entire surface. These gases make the small floating pieces of dry ice move in circles, or other directions, depending upon their shape. If the pieces of dry ice hit another solid object, such as a pair of tweezers or the side of a cup, the escaping gases push them away from the object.

Does liquid containing dry ice become carbonated? Would it be the same as a carbonated drink? How are carbonated drinks made?

When you drop a piece of dry ice into water, a small amount of the carbon dioxide gas that sublimes from the dry ice dissolves in the water, much like sugar (a solid) dissolves in water.

It's in there, even if you can't see it. The solution is commonly known as carbonated water. Carbonated water is also used in soft drinks, but it is prepared in a different way. The carbonated water in soft drinks has more dissolved carbon dioxide in it than you can get by dropping pieces of dry ice into water. The solubility of carbon dioxide in water depends on temperature and pressure. Carbon dioxide is more soluble at colder temperatures. You can observe this by sticking a hot spoon into a glass of cold soda. Carbon dioxide bubbles out vigorously near the spoon, where the liquid is warm and the carbon dioxide is less soluble. Carbon dioxide is also more soluble at higher pressures, like in a sealed soda bottle. You have probably observed this many times, simply by opening bottles of soda. You first hear a hiss as carbon dioxide gas that was pressurizing the bottle escapes. If you leave the cap off, the soda will "go flat." Commercial soft drinks are carbonated by bubbling carbon dioxide gas through the drink mix under high pressure (about 12 atm) and low temperature (about 5°C) conditions. The high pressure carbon dioxide gas comes from a metal tank that contains liquid carbon dioxide. It is not necessary to use solid carbon dioxide.

Does dry ice change the pH of the water it's in?

The carbon dioxide in water makes carbonic acid, which lowers the pH of the water, making it more acidic.

Why do drops of water slide off dry ice?

Small drops of water bounce off the cushions of carbon dioxide gas that surround the piece of dry ice as it sublimates.

How can a small piece of dry ice fill a large balloon?

Under typical conditions, **one gram** of carbon dioxide gas takes up about 2000 times more space than solid carbon dioxide (dry ice). It's not because the carbon dioxide molecules get bigger or break apart into more molecules. Rather, in the gas phase, carbon dioxide molecules are moving much faster than in the solid. Because they are moving faster, they take up more space. They have escaped the relatively small attractive forces that held them close together in the solid phase. If there is no container (plastic bag, balloon, soap bubble) to hold them, the carbon dioxide molecules will keep spreading—moving into a larger and larger volume.

Why does dry ice squeak when pressed against metal? Why does dry ice on a hot surface cause vibration and squeaking?

When you press a piece of dry ice against metal, carbon dioxide gas escaping through the small space between the dry ice and metal causes vibrations and various amusing squeaking noises. This is very similar to what happens when you squeeze a rubber ducky—the air escaping through a small hole causes cute squeaking noises! When you press dry ice against metal, you are pushing against the pressure of the escaping carbon dioxide gas. When these two forces exactly balance each other, the gliding hovercraft behavior results. But, when the forces alternately overcome each other, vibration and squeaking occur. This can happen when the surface is hot, or when you press hard, or both. When the dry ice touches the metal, the pressure of carbon dioxide gas increases at the point of contact, because metal conducts heat well. The escaping gas pushes the dry ice away from the metal, overcoming your efforts to push it toward the metal. However, when the dry ice is slightly away from the metal, the gas pressure is lower, because it is not being pressed on and because the dry ice is sublimating more slowly. Now, you are able to push the dry ice back towards the metal, overcoming the efforts of the escaping carbon dioxide gas to push it away from the metal. When the dry ice is back in contact with the metal, the gas pressure increases again. These events can repeat over and over again. You feel the motion of the piece of dry ice to and from the metal as vibration. You hear high frequency alternations in air pressure—due to the motion of the subliming dry ice and the vibrating metal—as sound. (If you do not have a rubber ducky, you can whistle a tune or make noises by clamping your hand tightly over your mouth and blowing. Both exercises illustrate the same process. Although the second kind of noise may sound rude, you can really feel the vibration and tickling where the air is escaping under your hand!)

Why doesn't water freeze when dry ice is added to it?
After all this fun with dry ice and water, you may be wondering why you did not make any water turn to ice. After all, the temperature of subliming dry ice is –78°C, much colder than 0°C, the freezing point of water. The answer lies in the amounts. You have been adding small amounts of dry ice to larger amounts of water. A small amount of heat energy is used to sublime the solid carbon dioxide and warm it up to the temperature of the water. This energy is removed from the water, cooling it. However, a much larger amount of heat energy must be removed from the water to cool it all down to 0°C to freeze it. A small amount of water on or next to dry ice will freeze to ice, and sometimes a layer of ice will form around a piece of dry ice.

Solids, Liquids, and Gases

Solids. In the solid state, objects have definite mass, volume, and shape, not dependent on their containers. A penny in a round jar, a square box, or a flat pocket always keeps its shape. If you heat a solid or press on it, the volume change is barely perceptible. In solids, the atoms or molecules are packed close together, usually in an ordered pattern (like marbles in a box). The forces that hold the atoms or molecules together are much stronger than their kinetic energy (energy of motion). As a result, the atoms and molecules in a solid vibrate in fixed positions, but do not move past each other.

Liquids. Liquids have a definite mass and volume, but they can change shape, and assume the shape of their container. Liquid water in a round jar is round; water in a square box is square; and if you try to put water in your pocket, it fits through the tiny holes in the

Solid substances can have a variety of other properties which depend on the actual chemical identities of the substances. Rock salts and ceramics are brittle; they break into little pieces when you drop them. Metals such as copper and aluminum are malleable; with effort, you can change their shapes. Metals are also good conductors of heat and electricity; insulators, such as wood, wax, or rubber, are not. Glass, diamonds, mica, and some plastics are transparent; granite, graphite, and iron are opaque. Gold, tin, sapphires, and chalk all have different colors.

Liquid substances can have a variety of other properties which depend on the actual chemical identities of the substances. Molasses, honey, and glycerin are viscous; they flow very slowly when you try to pour them. Alcohol and gasoline are much less viscous. Liquid metals, like mercury, are opaque, but you can see through water, vegetable oil, and most other liquids. Most common pure liquids are colorless or yellowish, but many solutions (homogeneous mixtures of liquids and other substances) can have brilliant colors. Some examples of colored solutions are grape juice and magic marker ink.

All gases are transparent, and most are colorless. You can't see air, helium, or carbon dioxide. A few gases are colored; nitrogen dioxide, found in smog, is brown. Iodine gas is purple. Many familiar gases, such as air (a mixture of several gases), natural gas, and steam, are odorless. Many others have distinctive odors; hydrogen sulfide gas smells like rotten eggs, methyl mercaptan is the odorant used in household natural gas, hydrogen cyanide gas smells like almonds, ethyl butyrate vapor smells like bananas, and phenylethyl acetate vapor smells like roses.

There are two other states of matter which are beyond the scope of this guide. One of these is plasma, which is found inside fluorescent light bulbs when they're on. Another is Einstein-Bose Condensate, a recently discovered phase that only occurs at near absolute zero temperatures.

fabric and runs down your leg. But, like solids, if you heat a liquid or press on it, the volume change is barely perceptible. The kinetic molecular theory explains why liquids have variable shapes but fixed volumes. The atoms or molecules in liquids are close together, but they are disordered and usually not as close together as in solids. Thus, the liquid form of most substances is less dense than the solid form. The kinetic energy of atoms and molecules in a liquid is greater than for the same substance as a solid, but still less than the forces that hold them together. In a liquid, the atoms and molecules tumble over each other; this allows the liquid to flow and mix with itself.

Gases. Gases have a definite mass, but no definite volume or shape. Gases can expand or contract to fill the shape and volume of almost any container. Air in a balloon is round; air in a square container is square; but you can't keep air in your pocket—it will always expand to fill the entire room, mixing with the other air. Gases are much less dense than either liquids or solids. Gas volume is very sensitive to temperature and pressure. If you heat a gas or squeeze it, the volume changes dramatically. Under typical conditions, one gram of a gas occupies about 1000 times the volume of one gram of liquid or solid. The kinetic molecular theory explains why gases have low densities and variable shapes and volumes. The atoms or molecules in a gas are very far apart. They move in straight lines in random directions until they collide with other gas particles or another object. The kinetic energy of atoms or molecules in a gas is so high that they escape from the forces that would hold them together in a liquid or solid. This allows the atoms or molecules to move around independently.

Phases and Phase Changes

What are phases?

Solids, liquids, and gases are three common states of matter, also called phases. You can sort almost every substance into these categories. Phases are determined by how fast the particles in a substance are moving, and how closely packed they are. Substances can change between these phases. When heat energy is added, the particles move more quickly and farther apart. When heat energy is taken away, the particles move more slowly and closer together.

What are phase changes?

Many substances can exist in more than one state. For example, ice, liquid water, and (invisible) steam are all different forms of the same substance, water (H_2O). Dry ice and carbon dioxide gas are both different forms of CO_2. Phase changes are physical processes in which one substance changes into a different form of the same substance.

How are phase changes affected by temperature?

You can cause phase changes by changing the temperature of a substance. If you heat a substance, you are adding energy; the atoms or molecules will gain kinetic energy and move faster. In this way, a solid will turn into liquid or a liquid turn to gas. If you decrease the temperature by cooling a substance, you are removing energy; the atoms or molecules will lose kinetic energy and move slower. In this way, a gas will turn into liquid or a liquid turn to solid. Different substances change phases at particular temperatures, which are characteristic properties of each substance. The following phase changes can occur:

Melting: SOLID + energy → LIQUID
Molecular level: Kinetic energy of molecules increases enough to overcome some, but not all, of the attractive forces that hold the solid together. Molecules begin to tumble over each other.
Example: Water ice melts at 0°C. Metallic iron melts at 1538°C.

Freezing: LIQUID → SOLID + energy
Molecular level: Kinetic energy of molecules decreases so much that the attractive forces hold them in fixed positions.
Example: Liquid water freezes at 0°C. Liquid iron freezes at 1538°C (when it's still hot!).

Boiling: LIQUID + energy → GAS
Molecular level: Kinetic energy of molecules increases enough to escape all of the attractive forces that hold the liquid together. Molecules move into whatever space is available.
Example: Water boils at 100°C. Liquid nitrogen boils at –196°C (when it's very cold!).

Condensation: GAS → LIQUID + energy
Molecular level: Kinetic energy of molecules decreases so much that they are captured by attractive forces and stick together.
Example: Steam condenses to liquid water at 100°C. Nitrogen gas from air condenses at –196°C.

Sublimation: SOLID + energy → GAS
Molecular level: Kinetic energy of molecules increases enough to escape all of the attractive forces that hold the solid together. Molecules move into whatever space is available.
Example: Solid carbon dioxide (dry ice) sublimes at –78°C. Other examples of sublimation: iodine, water ice in a freezer may sublime.

Deposition: GAS → SOLID + energy
Molecular level: Kinetic energy of molecules decreases so much that they are captured by attractive forces and stick together in fixed positions.
Example: Carbon dioxide deposits at –78°C.

Can you cause a phase change by changing the pressure?

Changing the temperature is not the only way to cause phase changes. Liquids and solids have high density and gases have low density. You can make gases turn into liquids (condensation) or solid (deposition) by squeezing them (increasing pressure). If you lower the pressure, you can also make liquids boil or evaporate, or solids sublimate. Simply changing the pressure does not, however, satisfy all the energy requirements for a phase change. If you squeeze a gas, it will condense to liquid, energy will still be released from the gas, and it would make you feel warm. If you remove pressure from a liquid by expanding its container, it will evaporate to gas, energy is still required by the liquid, and its loss would make you feel cool. This is the basic idea used in refrigerators. The coolant inside a refrigerator changes back and forth between a liquid and a gas. The motor compresses the gas coolant into a liquid, and energy is released. This energy is the warmth you can feel behind the refrigerator. The cool liquid then flows into a long tube inside the refrigerator. Inside the tube, the pressure is lower because the tube is large. Because there's less pressure, the liquid coolant evaporates to a gas, but it needs energy to do this. It takes this energy from things inside the refrigerator, cooling them. Then the gaseous coolant flows back to the compressor, where the cycle begins all over again.

As you and your class have seen, at normal atmospheric pressure (1 atm) dry ice changes from a solid to a gas. It changes to a liquid only at pressures above 5.1 atmospheres. It actually is possible to create this amount of pressure in the classroom and thus see carbon dioxide in its liquid form. The best procedure we have seen for this is found in *Investigating Solids, Liquids, and Gases with TOYS: States of Matter and Changes of State* (see the "Resources" section for publication information). The procedure is described and illustrated in the chapter entitled "The Phase Changes of Carbon Dioxide," which begins on page 219. It requires the use of wide-stem polyethylene Beral pipets with powdered dry ice placed in the bulb, a pair of pliers, a ziplock bag, gloves or tongs, goggles, and other accessible materials. The gas released by the powdered dry ice builds up the pressure inside the pipet. This makes it possible for students to see the remaining dry ice liquefy, then, when the grip on the pliers is loosened, to see it re-solidify as the pressure decreases. This can be repeated several times, but takes considerable practice. At the end of the procedure the pressure is allowed to build to where the pipet bursts safely, with the bulb held in water.

A phase diagram is a helpful way to visualize how the factors of both temperature and pressure affect the phase changes of substances. To the left is a phase change diagram for carbon dioxide. As you can see, at a pressure of 1 atm and a temperature below −78°C, carbon dioxide exists as a solid. At a temperature above −78°C and less than 5.1 atm pressure, it is a gas. At a pressure above 5.1 atm solid carbon dioxide will melt into a liquid when its temperature increases.

Phase change diagram for carbon dioxide

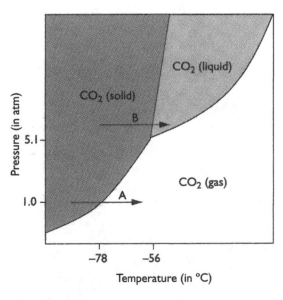

Line A represents the sublimation of solid carbon dioxide at 1 atm as it is warmed above −78°C. This represents the usual change of state for solid carbon dioxide at normal pressure. Line B shows that at a pressure above 5.1 atm, solid carbon dioxide will melt into a liquid when its temperature increases.

Particulate Model of Matter

Why do scientists believe that all matter is made up of atoms?

Atoms are very tiny particles that cannot be created or destroyed by chemical means. Imagine starting with a full glass of water, and pouring out half, and then pouring out half of what was left, and then pouring out half again... If the current scientific idea of atoms is correct, you could divide the water in half some 85 times. Then you'd have one water molecule. You could use electricity to divide it into one oxygen atom and two hydrogen atoms.

In the early 19th century (1807) Dalton became intrigued with the idea of atoms because it explained a very interesting observation. The elements only combine to form compounds in certain whole number ratios. For example, from hydrogen and oxygen atoms, you can only make two stable substances, water (H_2O) and hydrogen peroxide (H_2O_2). From carbon and oxygen, you can make carbon monoxide (CO) and carbon dioxide (CO_2).

Toward the end of the 19th century, scientists began to get an idea of atomic size. Two researchers, Lord Rayleigh in England and Agnes Pockels in Germany, observed the properties of oil films floating on water. Drops of oil only spread out so far, until they have a certain minimum thickness. If oil really is made up of molecules, themselves made of carbon, hydrogen, and oxygen atoms, it was thought this experiment might reveal the size of the oil molecules. The thickness of the oil films turned out to be on the order of nanometers (billionths of a meter). It is now thought that the actual atoms are about 10 times smaller than that!

Nobody has ever seen an individual atom. Today, scientists say that we can "see" individual atoms, using various techniques such as mass spectrometry and scanning tunneling microscopy (STM). Using the current understanding of atoms, complicated electrical signals resulting from mass spectrometers and STM experiments can be predicted and explained. It's not that we can really see atoms now. It's that so many experiments support the idea of atoms, that science is close to 100% confident in the atomic theory.

There are more than 100 different kinds of atoms (the different kinds of atoms are called elements, such as oxygen and hydrogen). The elements are all numbered and organized on the Periodic Table. The vast numbers of different substances on earth are made from different combinations of elements. Careful observations of many chemical reactions has provided evidence for the elements and for the elemental composition of many substances. Even though we can't see them, we have surmised from a great deal of evidence and included as part of the particulate model of matter that atoms and molecules are moving. One way to begin considering this is if you open a bottle of perfume on one side of a room, eventually the molecules will drift across to the other side where someone will be able to smell it. A second way is to observe the mixing of liquid solutions. If you add a drop of food coloring to a glass of water, the color will eventually be homogeneous, even if you don't stir the water. The dye and water molecules must be moving in order to mix. A third way is to watch larger objects move around when molecules collide with them. The random motions of dust particles in the air, which can be observed in a shaft of sunlight coming through a window, has been ascribed to collisions with fast moving air molecules.

What is temperature at the atomic or molecular level?

The temperature of a substance that we feel or measure is the average kinetic energy of the molecules. At the macroscopic level, we can feel when different objects have different temperatures. Our perception of temperature is related to the flow of energy between objects and our skin. When an object feels warm to us, energy is flowing out of the object into our hand. When an object feels cool to us, energy is flowing out of our hand into the object. When any warmer object is in contact with a cooler object, energy will flow from the warm object to the cool object, until they eventually reach the same temperature. At the molecular level, moving atoms and molecules have kinetic energy, or energy of motion. Faster molecules have more kinetic energy than slower ones with the same mass. Kinetic energy is transferred between molecules when they collide. A collection of fast moving molecules will have a higher average temperature than a collection of slow molecules. When we touch something that feels cold to us, the average kinetic energy of the molecules in our skin is greater than that in the cold object. Something that feels warm to us has a higher average kinetic energy of the molecules than our skin.

What is pressure, and what causes it at the molecular level?

When you put a piece of dry ice in a sealed balloon, it sublimes into carbon dioxide gas, and the balloon inflates. The molecules in the gas are constantly crashing into each other and the inner "walls" of the balloon. These collisions cause pressure. In the same way, inside a bicycle tire, the air molecules are constantly colliding with each other and with the tire walls. These collisions happen individually as separate events, but they happen so frequently, the tire gauge measures a continuous pressure. The pressure we measure is the average force of all the individual collisions in a certain area over a certain time.

Why does a helium balloon deflate overnight, but a carbon dioxide or oxygen balloon doesn't?

Rubber balloons filled with helium deflate quickly because helium atoms are small enough to fit through many of the tiny holes in the rubber. Carbon dioxide and oxygen molecules are about twice as large and about 10 times as heavy as helium atoms. Because of their larger size, carbon dioxide and oxygen molecules do not fit through as many of the holes in the rubber. Because of their larger mass, they move slower than the helium atoms. Balloons made out of Mylar have become popular because they can hold helium better than rubber balloons.

DRY ICE CRYSTALS SEEN FOR FIRST TIME!!!!

Scientists have only been able to actually see carbon dioxide crystals since 1998! The crystals usually evaporate at temperatures higher than −134°C (−210°F). In 1998, William P. Wergin and his colleagues at the U.S. Agricultural Research Service (ARS) were able to view the extremely tiny crystals, which are as small as 1/200,000 of an inch. The crystals generally appear as eight-sided structures, or octahedrons. The scientists (who originally were investigating the structure of snowflakes, with much larger crystals than those of carbon dioxide) used a special low-temperature scanning electron microscope (SEM) to view the carbon dioxide crystals, cooling the stage of the microscope to −320°F. The results were highly magnified images such as the one shown here.

It is thought that increased scientific understanding of the structure of carbon dioxide may be helpful in understanding why dry ice crystals are effective in seeding clouds for rainfall. More globally, scientists also hope that knowing more about the crystalline structure will provide clues to the capacity of carbon dioxide gas to absorb and re-radiate energy and thus help them learn more about the greenhouse effect and measures that can be taken to reduce global warming. The research also has great potential for interplanetary studies, especially a better understanding of Mars, whose polar ice caps are made up of both frozen water and frozen carbon dioxide (dry ice). ARS scientists are collaborating with NASA scientists to see if the SEM technology used in viewing the crystals can be adapted to future studies of the surface of Mars. For more on these interesting matters, visit the ARS web site at:

www.ars.usda.gov/is/pr/1998/980223.b.htm

and/or

www.ars.usda.gov/is/AR/archive/oct98/crys1098.htm

Research on Student Ideas:
Blueberry Muffins and Other Misconceptions

There is a large body of research on the ideas relating to science that students of different ages bring with them into the classroom. A number of these studies relate to concepts that are raised by the investigations in this unit, including the particulate theory of matter, phase change, and the nature and behavior of gases.

The often mistaken or incomplete ideas that student bring with them are sometimes called "misconceptions" when they are not accurate. In some cases, they are called "preconceptions" to indicate that they precede more evolved concepts. Other educators prefer to use the term "alternate conceptions" to give value to the ideas that students have worked out for themselves, which, although they may not be fully accurate, are often complex, and part of an extensive mental framework developed over time.

In this section, we summarize briefly some of these ideas, so you can be alert to student thinking as you proceed through the unit. Having a sense of possible misconceptions is helpful in many ways, for example, when you assess student understanding. As you develop questioning strategies to gauge the depth of student comprehension and encourage students to explain their reasoning, it is likely that some of these ideas may crop up. Having students draw or diagram what they think is happening can also reveal their underlying ideas. It is important to emphasize that research has shown conclusively that such "alternate conceptions" take time and multiple experiences to be transformed into more accurate understandings. People do not part easily from their previous understandings. Successive experiences over time are often required, of greater complexity from grade to grade, especially working with substances, phenomena, or models that behave in ways that cause students to confront their previous interpretations. Reflection upon these discrepant experiences and discussions in which alternate points of view are raised can also be instrumental in student development of more accurate conceptions. It is our hope that, in relation to at least some of the misconceptions summarized below, the experiences and reflections in *Dry Ice Investigations* will provide some important steps along your students' paths to improved understanding.

Children's Ideas in Science

Children's Ideas in Science (edited by Driver, Guesne, and Tiberghien, 1985) contains several chapters that examine topics raised by this unit, especially Chapters 6, 7, and 8, on gases, the particulate nature of matter, and the conservation of matter. Chapter 7, by Joseph Nussbaum, begins, "One of the central instructional goals of most junior high school curricula is the understanding by pupils of the particulate nature of matter. For, in modern science, the fundamental notion that all matter is particulate and not continuous is of prime importance for all causal explanations of any kind of change in matter." Nussbaum then analyzes four studies in three different countries, Israel, England, and the United States. He examines the underlying logical and "common sense" concepts underlying the history of human ideas about the structure of matter. While the studies show the "tenacious nature" of student preconceptions, the article is not pessimistic and instead strongly advocates for more effective teaching strategies that take into account the major misconceptions and provide students with experiences that cause them to revise their earlier ideas. Some of Nussbaum's specific findings are mentioned below—the book itself is highly recommended as one of the best summaries of what is known about student's initial ideas on major scientific concepts.

A number of studies (Bodner, 1992; Lee et al., 1993; Stavy, 1990) highlight the difficulty of developing student abilities to reconcile the macroscopic and molecular worlds, and to further align these understandings with chemical symbols. Many students, for example, learn to use "molecular language" but "retain basic misconceptions they had prior to instruction" (Lee et al., 1993). Several studies emphasize the need to start out with an observation, experience, or concept that is accessible to students, and build toward the more abstract.

In several different studies, students of different ages were found to believe that matter is continuous, rather than being made up of particles (Nakleh, 1992; Novick and Nussbaum, 1981; Lee et al., 1993). Interestingly, those students who did have some understanding of molecules had a tendency to view molecules as being embedded in a substance, rather than fully making up that substance, a misconception that Lee et al. characterized as like "blueberries in a muffin." Many students did not visualize empty space between molecules, even in a gas.

Molecules and Phase Change

In terms of molecules themselves, a range of student misconceptions has been noted. In one study, students viewed molecules as solid spheres, with no space within them (Griffiths and Preston, 1992). The same study revealed confusion about the size of molecules, including statements such as, "they are about the size of a piece of dust." Forty percent of the students tested thought that water molecules contained components other than oxygen and hydrogen and that the composition of the molecules depended on temperature and phase. In some cases students thought that molecules changed size during a phase change. Some thought the largest molecules would be found in ice; others that heat would make molecules larger (Griffiths and Preston, 1992; Lee et al., 1993). Some students further believed that the shape of a container could affect the size of molecules, that molecules might have macroscopic properties, such as color or taste, and even that molecules could be "alive" (de Vos and Verdonk, 1996).

As regards changes of state, or phase change, one of the key aspects in this unit, while students generally did understand that matter exists in different states, there was confusion among younger (sixth grade) students as to whether gas was a form of matter or energy. Some students, for example, classified liquids and solids as forms of matter and gas as a form of energy. In some cases, students attributed changes in states of matter to the molecules themselves. Since students in many of the studies had not yet developed their understanding to think in terms of matter as composed of particles with space between them, they were not able to view phase changes as a change in the *arrangement* of molecules (Stavy, 1990; Lee et al., 1993).

Both Lee et al. (1993) and Benson et al. (1993) found that students had a number of misconceptions concerning the nature and behavior of gases, including the belief that gases flow like liquids and are unevenly distributed within a container. Many students believed that there is little or no space between molecules in a gas—that the gas is continuous. Some also believe that gas is weightless or that it weighs less than a solid (Stavy, 1990). Stavy found that by seventh grade students were able to conserve the weight of iodine and acetone gas and that many students could explain that "the molecules only got further apart." At the same time, Lee et al. (1993) found that "understanding the conservation of matter, particularly water vapor in the air, turned out to be the most difficult of all the macroscopic conceptions for students." Stavy (1990) found that only about half of seventh grade students understood conservation of matter during evaporation.

There have been many other studies of young children's ideas about evaporation. Bar and Travis (1991) found that, at about the age of nine, understanding of evaporation begins to improve. Before that misconceptions abound, including those who believed the water "disappeared," those who thought the remaining water represented a condensed form of the original water (conserving mass but not volume) and those who believed that the liquid had somehow penetrated into solid objects and was therefore no longer visible. Additional studies by Bar and Galili (1994) conclude that the conceptual change of view on evaporation is clearly correlated with cognitive development, as well as with student progress in operative knowledge—their use of the conservation principle and ability to adopt an abstract model for air. To the extent that issues related to evaporation may also apply to sublimation, these studies suggest that students may also experience difficulty in fully understanding and accurately explaining what is happening when dry ice sublimes. This also suggests that, if dry ice activities are adapted for lower grades, younger students should not be expected to be able to construct more abstract ideas relating to the particulate nature of matter or the kinetic molecular behavior of gases.

Bar, V. and Galili, I. Stages of children's views about evaporation, *International Journal of Science Education*, Vol. 16, No. 2, pages 157–174, 1994.

Bar, V. and Travis, A.S. Children's views concerning phase change, *Journal of Research in Science Teaching*, Vol. 28, No. 4, pages 363–382, 1991.

Benson, D.L., Wittrock, M.C., Baur, M. Students Preconceptions of the Nature of Gases, *Journal of Research in Science Teaching*, Vol. 30, No. 6, pages 587–597, 1993.

Bodner, G.M. Why Changing the Curriculum May Not Be Enough, *Journal of Chemical Education*, Vol. 69, No. 3, pages 186–190, 1992.

de Vos, W. and Verdonk, A.H. The Particulate Nature of Matter in Science Education and in Science, *Journal of Research in Science Teaching*, Vol. 33, No. 6, pages 657–664, 1996.

Driver, R., Guesne E., Tiberghien, A. (editors) *Children's Ideas in Science*, Open University Press/ Milton Keynes, Philadelphia, 1985.

Furio Mas, C.J., Hernandez Perez, J., Harris, H.H. Parallels between Adolescent's Conception of Gases and the History of Chemistry, *Journal of Chemical Education*, Vol. 64, No. 7, pages 616–618, 1987.

Griffiths, A.K. and Preston, K.R. Grade 12 Students' Misconceptions Relating to Fundamental Characteristics of Atoms and Molecules, *Journal of Research in Science Teaching*, Vol. 29, No. 6, pages 611–628, 1992.

Lee, O., Eichinger, D.C., Anderson, C.W., Berkheimer, G.D., Blakeslee, T.D. Changing Middle School Students' Conceptions of Matter and Molecules, *Journal of Research in Science Teaching*, Vol. 30, No. 3, pages 249–270, 1993.

McGooey, J.P. Pairing and Compiling Discrepant Events to Help Generate Understanding of Kinetic Molecular Theory, *Proceedings of the Fourth International Misconceptions Seminar*, Meaningful Learning Research Group, Cornell University, Ithaca, New York, 1997.

Nakleh, M.B. Students' Models of Matter in the Context of Acid-Base Chemistry, *Proceedings of the Third International Seminar on Misconceptions and Educational Strategies in Science and Mathematics*, Misconceptions Trust, Cornell University, Ithaca, New York, 1993.

Nakleh, M.B. Why Some Students Don't Learn Chemistry: Chemical Misconceptions, *Journal of Chemistry Education*, Vol. 69, No. 3, pages 191–196, 1992.

Novick, S. and Nussbaum, J. Junior high school pupils' understanding of the particulate nature of matter. An interview study, *Science Education*, Vol. 62, pages 273–281, 1978.

Novick, S. and Nussbaum, J. Pupils' understanding of the particulate nature of matter. A cross-age study, *Science Education*, Vol. 65, No. 2, pages 187–196, 1981.

Skelly, K. The Development and Validation of a Categorization of Sources of Misconceptions in Chemistry, *Proceedings of the Third International Seminar on Misconceptions and Educational Strategies in Science and Mathematics*, Misconceptions Trust, Cornell University, Ithaca, New York, 1993.

Sneider, C. and Ohadi, M. Unravelling Students' Misconceptions About the Earth's Shape and Gravity, *Science Education*, Vol. 82, pages 265–284, 1998.

Sneider, C. with Bar, V. and Martimbeau, N. What Research Says: Is There Gravity in Space? *Science and Children*, April 1997.

Sneider, C. with Bar, V., Zinn, B., Goldmuntz, R. Children's Concepts About Weight and Free Fall, *Science Education*, Vol. 78, No. 2, pages 149–169, 1994.

Stavy, R. Pupils' problems in understanding conservation of matter, *International Journal of Science Education*, Vol. 12, No. 5, pages 501–512, 1990.

Stavy, R. Using analogy to overcome misconceptions about the conservation of matter, *Journal of Research in Science Teaching*, Vol. 28, No. 4, pages 305–313, 1991.

Tveita, J. Constructivistic Teaching Methods Helping Students to Develop Particle Models in Science, *Proceedings of the Fourth International Misconceptions Seminar*, Meaningful Learning Research Group, Cornell University, Ithaca, New York, 1997.

Tveita, J. Helping Middle School Students to Learn the Kinetic Particle Model, *Proceedings of the Third International Seminar on Misconceptions and Educational Strategies in Science and Mathematics*, Misconceptions Trust, Cornell University, Ithaca, New York, 1993.

Whiteley, P. Caribbean High School Students' Conceptions of the Kinetic Model of Matter, *Proceedings of the Third International Seminar on Misconceptions and Educational Strategies in Science and Mathematics*, Misconceptions Trust, Cornell University, Ithaca, New York, 1993.

Inquiry and Scaffolding:
Cross Over That Bridge

As the introductory sections for this guide make clear, a major focus of this unit is growth in student ability to engage in inquiry. This has been a central goal since its beginnings, further strengthened by the strong emphasis on open inquiry and full investigation in the *National Science Education Standards*, and by the results of the intensive GEMS process of classroom trial testing. (We also needed to fit the inquiry experiences of the unit into limitations imposed by what is available in the average classroom. For some kinds of experiments with gases, for example, sophisticated laboratory equipment would be required, and we wanted to remain with the trademarked GEMS goal of accessibility for all students and classrooms!)

At all phases of the unit's development, teachers and students were enthusiastic and we received many "rave reviews." A number of teachers, however, raised a significant concern. They agreed that the early versions of the unit succeeded admirably in the goal of getting students involved in explorations (with a great assist from the marvelous attributes of dry ice!) and in that way involved students directly in the delving into the nature of science (similar to the GEMS *Oobleck* unit). However, when it came to students designing their own investigations, in many cases student work did not progress much further than their initial explorations. If the unit were to truly help students develop their inquiry abilities more fully, we realized that there was a crucial bridge to cross and that earlier versions had not provided sufficient foundation. Students and teachers needed to be provided with more support—more **scaffolding**—upon which to build their investigations. For this reason, we added major new components to the unit that include: emphasis on investigable questions; modeling of possible investigation approaches; clear working definitions of experiments and systematic observations; and careful attention and considerable practice given to the planning process—all seen as part of the overall investigation or inquiry process.

Articles and comments by Wynn Harlan were of great assistance to us in considering the important role that the selection of a question plays in launching (and sustaining) an investigation. In a chapter on children's questions she classifies questions into a number of categories, including "questions which can lead to investigation by children." She continues:

'Turning' questions into investigable ones is an important skill since it enables teachers to treat difficult questions seriously but without providing answers beyond children's understanding. It also indicates to children that they can go a long way to finding answers through their own investigation, thus underlining the implicit messages about the nature of scientific activity and their ability to answer questions by 'asking the objects.' (Harlan, 1996)

Harlan's careful analysis of the need for student practice in planning an investigation was also of crucial assistance. She points out that planning begins from the initial raising of a question or posing of a problem. The posing of a problem may or may not be expressed in a way that opens up an investigation. So the first step is to pose the problem as a question that can be investigated. Once the question is focused, the next step is to consider, from the standpoint of experimentation, what factors need to remain the same, which will be changed, and what outcome or effects will provide the results. When the planning group has clarified this, the next step in planning is to work out the specifics of the experiment. Among strategies that teachers have found most helpful in communicating the importance of planning are: (1) encouraging groups of students to work together to come up with experimental plans; (2) providing a basic structure to help students guide their planning; and (3) making sure to discuss, after the investigation, not only the results, but also the original plan and how it might have been improved. This review of what was done is not only very helpful in teaching students to improve their planning of experiments in the future, it also helps them revisit what they learned in general and so contributes to constructing their new understandings. (Harlan, 1985)

Another important influence in our revision work on inquiry came about through our communication with Anthony Cody, an Oakland teacher who had worked with the Full Option Science System (FOSS) program at the Lawrence Hall of Science, and who had used dry ice activities in designing classroom research for his master's thesis (Cody, 1998). In his thesis, Cody asks the central question: "How can we create a framework for inquiry that provides the guidance students need, yet allows their questions to drive their investigations?" Cody used two models for inquiry, one which he called open-ended inquiry and the other which he termed guided inquiry. His analysis of the open-ended inquiry model, which involved exploration of a science kit of materials, found that most students, although urged to come up with investigable questions and an experiment, did not move past the exploration phase. In contrast, the guided-inquiry model, in which the class generated observations and questions together, student groups worked to refine questions and plans for an experiment, and the teacher reviewed student investigation plans to place them in a lab activity format, was much more successful in taking students through the entire process. Cody adds, "The guided-investigation model thus provided a scaffold from which understanding of the scientific process was built." His work was thus supportive of our efforts to provide an underpinning of support to students, while not sacrificing a sense of student "ownership" of their own questions and investigations.

While providing this scaffolding throughout the *Dry Ice Investigations* unit, we also sought to avoid a kind of "lockstep" version of the experimental process. Rather than focus only on controlled experimentation, for example, we included systematic observation, and we endeavored to emphasize the flexible nature of scientific investigation in the real world, which often combines many elements of the inquiry process in creative ways, depending on the substance or phenomena being explored. In this we found instructive some investigation categories described in the New Standards™ Elementary Science Portfolio, which includes overhead summaries of: Experiment; Systematic Observation; Design; and Research. We also found instructive a student data sheet devised by Jonathan Cohen, a science teacher in the Berkeley public schools, who helped us trial test the final version of the unit.

The following summary table reflects the basic elements of the "scaffolding" we have provided in *Dry Ice Investigations* to encourage, develop, strengthen, and sustain inquiry:

The "Scaffolding" in Dry Ice Investigations

Scaffolding: Experiences that prepare students to be able to successfully conduct independent full inquiries/investigations.

Activity 1: Observing/Wondering
- Experience making objective observations and comparisons
- Take on a scientist's mindset by wondering why and making no assumptions
- Learn that good scientists (and good thinkers!) revise their explanations based on new data

Activity 2: Exploration/Systematic Observation
- Opportunity for free exploration
- Experience systematic observation
- Compare the relative power of different ways of finding out (exploration vs. systematic observation)
- Practice in wondering why
- Encouragement to take risk of suggesting an explanation
- Increase the care and rigor with which explanations are made

Activity 3: Experimenting

- Distinguish between systematic observation and experiments

- Introduce concepts of test and outcome variables

- Be guided through an experiment

- Practice drawing conclusions

- Gain experience determining the outcome variable and how to quantify results

Activity 4: Planning and Conducting an Investigation

- Gain experience distinguishing between investigable questions and non-investigable questions

- Be guided in how to choose the appropriate investigation path

- Practice identifying variables

- Have the opportunity to conduct and refine an investigation

- Use careful reasoning to make sense of the data and draw conclusions

---

There is a large (and growing) body of work on inquiry in science and science teaching; the following references were most helpful to us in revising the unit.

American Association for the Advancement of Science. *Benchmarks for Science Literacy,* Oxford University Press, New York, 1993.

Cody, A. "Student Questions: Foundations for Inquiry," Master's Thesis to Faculty of the College of Education, San Jose State University, 1998.

Driver, R. The construction of scientific knowledge in school classrooms, In R. Miller (editor) *Doing science: Images of science in science education,* Falmer Press, New York, 1989.

Flick, L.B. Integrating Elements of Inquiry into the Flow of Middle Level Teaching, Annual Meeting of the National Association for Research in Science Teaching, San Diego, April 19–22, 1998.

Harlen, W. (editor) *Primary Science: Taking the Plunge: How to teach primary science more effectively,* Heinemann Educational Publishers, Oxford, 1985. (See especially Chapter 4, "The Right Question at the Right Time," by Jos Eltgeest; Chapter 5, "Helping Children Raise Questions—and Answering Them," by Sheila Jelly; and Chapter 6, "Helping Children To Plan Investigations," by Wynne Harlen.)

Harlen, W. *The Teaching of Science in Primary Schools,* David Fulton, London, 1996. (See especially Chapter 14, "Encouraging Children's Questions" and Chapter 15, "Handling Children's Questions.")

National Research Council. *National Science Education Standards,* National Academy Press, Washington, D.C., 1996.

National Center on Education and the Economy and the University of Pittsburgh, New Standards Project. *Performance Standards, Volume 1, Elementary School,* 1997.

Polman, J. and Pea, R. Scaffolding Science Inquiry Through Transformative Communication, Annual Meeting of the National Association for Research in Science Teaching, Oak Brook, Illinois, March 1997.

Rakow, S. J. *Teaching science as inquiry,* Phi Delta Kappa Educational Foundation, Bloomington, Indiana, 1986.

Rutherford, F. J. and Ahlgren, A. *Science for All Americans,* Oxford University Press, New York, 1990.

Sneider, C., Kurlich, K., Pulos, S., Friedman, A. Learning to Control Variables with Model Rockets: A Neo-Piagetian Study of Learning in Field Settings, *Science Education,* Vol. 68, No. 4, pages 463–484, 1984.

Sneider, C. and Ohadi, M. Unravelling Students' Misconceptions About the Earth's Shape and Gravity, *Science Education,* Vol. 82, pages 265–284, 1998.

Resources

Sources for Materials

Dry Ice

The ABC Ice House
www.dryiceInfo.com

700 places to purchase dry ice
in the United States and lots
of other information

Acme Dry Ice Co.
100 Kirkland St.
Cambridge, MA 02138
(617) 547-7300   or   (888) ACMEICE

Will ship to all of Massachusetts.

Airgas Dry Ice
Penguin Brand

Distributes dry ice to thousands of grocery stores
coast to coast.
Call 1-877-PENGUIN for the location nearest you.

New England Dry Ice Co.
P.O. Box 4606
Manchester, NH 03108
(603) 668-3448   or   (800) 544-1012
http://www.newenglanddryice.com

Will ship to the following New England states:
Massachusetts, Maine, New Hampshire, and
Vermont.

Polar Dry Ice
510 West 8th St.
Lansdale, PA 19446
(215) 361-7700

Will ship to all of Pennsylvania.

Dry Ice Keepers, Dry Ice Makers, and Dry Ice Machines

All of these items may be obtained from the scientific supply companies listed below.
The dry ice keepers are extra thick (approx. 1 ½") expanded polystyrene coolers/ice
chests. The dry ice makers produce flaked snow-like dry ice. The dry ice machines make
blocks of dry ice. The machines are expensive, but may be worthwhile if many classes in
your school or schools in your district are conducting dry ice activities. Both the dry ice
makers and machines require the attachment of a CO_2 cylinder.

Carolina Biological Supply Company
P.O. Box 6010
Burlington, NC 27216-6010
(800) 334-5551

Fisher Science Education
485 South Frontage Road
Burr Ridge, IL 60521
(800) 955-1177

Frey Scientific
Beckley Cardy Group
100 Paragon Parkway
Mansfield, OH 44903
(888) 222-1332

Science Kit & Boreal Laboratories
777 East Park Drive
Tonawanda, NY 14150-6784
(800) 828-7777

VWR Scientific/Sargent-Welch
911 Commerce Court
Buffalo Grove, IL 60089-2375
(800) 727-4368

Books

Adventures with Atoms and Molecules: Chemistry Experiments for Young People, Robert C. Mebane and Thomas R. Rybolt, (in the Adventures with Science series), Enslow, Hillside, New Jersey, 1985.
Chemistry experiments for home or school demonstrate the properties and behavior of various kinds of atoms and molecules. Concepts covered include properties of molecules, how temperature affects the behavior of molecules, and how the molecules in different liquids act.

Adventures with Atoms and Molecules, Book II: Chemistry Experiments for Young People, Robert C. Mebane and Thomas R. Rybolt, (in the Adventures with Science series), Enslow, Hillside, New Jersey, 1987.

Adventures with Atoms and Molecules, Book III: Chemistry Experiments for Young People, Robert C. Mebane and Thomas R. Rybolt, (in the Adventures with Science series), Enslow, Hillside, New Jersey, 1991.

Adventures with Atoms and Molecules, Book IV: Chemistry Experiments for Young People, Robert C. Mebane and Thomas R. Rybolt, (in the Adventures with Science series), Enslow, Hillside, New Jersey, 1992.

Air and Other Gases, Robert Mebane and Thomas Rybolt, (in the Everyday Material Science Experiments series), Twenty-First Century Books, New York, 1995.

Asimov's Chronology of Science and Discovery, Isaac Asimov, Harper & Row, New York, 1989.

Between Fire and Ice: The Science of Heat, David Darling, Silver Burdett Press, New York, 1992.
A collection of experiments exploring heat and its effects.

Experiments with Chemistry, Helen J. Challand, Childrens Press, Chicago, 1988.
A brief introduction to chemistry, discussing atoms, molecules, the periodic chart, chemical changes, and states of matter. Includes simple experiments.

From Glasses to Gases: The Science of Matter, David Darling, (in the Experiment! series), Silver Burdett Press, New York, 1992.
Text and experiments introduce matter and the various forms it can take under different conditions.

Fun with Chemistry: A Guidebook of K–12 Activities, M. Sarquis and J. Sarquis, Editors, Institute for Chemical Education, Madison, Wisconsin, 1993.

A Handbook to the Universe: Explorations of Matter, Energy, Space, and Time for Beginning Scientific Thinkers, Richard Paul, Chicago Review, Chicago, 1993.
Provides a great deal of background information on matter, as well as some history of scientific investigations into the topic.

How to Think Like a Scientist: Answering Questions by the Scientific Method, Stephen P. Kramer, T.Y. Crowell, New York, 1987.
Uses questions about hypothetical situations to introduce the process of thinking according to the scientific method.

Ideas for Science Projects, Robert Gardner, (in the Experimental Science series), F. Watts, New York, 1986.
Introduces the scientific method through instructions for observations and experiments in biology, physics, astronomy, botany, psychology, and chemistry.

Investigating Solids, Liquids, and Gases with TOYS: States of Matter and Changes of State, Jerry Sarquis, Lynn Hogue, Mickey Sarquis, and Linda Woodward, Terrific Science Press/McGraw-Hill, New York, 1997.
Includes 24 physical science activities for middle school grades. This book helps teachers provide opportunities for their students to explore matter in its three states, to compare and contrast the properties of the states, and to determine the conditions necessary for matter to change from one state to another.

It's a Gas!, Margaret Griffin and Ruth Griffin, Kids Can Press, Toronto, 1993.

Teaches all about gases with dozens of hands-on activities. Looks at the properties of gases, their relationship to liquids and solids, how they work in the human body, how they provide light, heat, and refrigeration, and their roles in the earth's environment.

Janice VanCleave's Molecules, Janice VanCleave, (in the Spectacular Science Projects series), John Wiley & Sons, New York, 1993.

A collection of science experiments and projects exploring molecules.

Make It Change, David Evans and Claudette Williams, (in the Let's Explore Science series), Dorling Kindersley, New York, 1992.

Uses simple observations and experiments to explore how various materials are changed by such processes as heating, wetting, and stirring.

Matter, Christopher Cooper, (in the Eyewitness Science series), Dorling Kindersley, New York, 1992.

Examines the elements that make up the physical world and the properties and behavior of different kinds of matter.

Matter and Energy, Robert Friedhoffer, F. Watts, New York, 1992.

Experiments, magic tricks, and other activities explore the scientific principles of matter and energy.

Molecules and Heat, Robert Friedhoffer, F. Watts, New York, 1992.

Experiments, magic tricks, and other activities explore the scientific principles of molecules and heat.

More Ideas for Science Projects, Robert Gardner, (in the Experimental Science series), F. Watts, New York, 1989.

Presents ideas for an exploration of how to set up science projects in the areas of astronomy, ecology, energy, biology, anatomy, botany, physics, and engineering.

Science Mini-Mysteries, Sandra Markle, Simon & Schuster, New York, 1988.

Provides instructions for 29 scientific experiments, tricks, and effects, in which the reader is challenged to explain or predict the final outcome.

Science Projects About Chemistry, Robert Gardner, (in the Science Projects series), Enslow, Hillside, New Jersey, 1994.

Science to the Rescue, Sandra Markle, Simon & Schuster, New York, 1994.

Presents ways science is being used today to meet problems such as the necessity for precision surgery, atmospheric pollution, and overpopulation of coastal cities. Provides hands-on projects for the reader and stresses the importance of the scientific method.

Scienceworks: 65 Experiments that Introduce the Fun and Wonder of Science, from the Ontario Science Centre, Addison-Wesley, Reading, Massachusetts, 1986.

Provides instructions for experiments that reveal a variety of scientific principles.

The Scientist Within You: Experiments and Biographies of Distinguished Women in Science, Rebecca L. Warren and Mary H. Thompson, (in the Scientist Within You series), ACI (Alpha Communications Inc.) Publishing, Eugene, Oregon, 1996.

An instructor's guide for use with ages 8 through 13 includes 25 Discovery units with hands-on experiments and activities based on the work of 23 women scientists and mathematicians.

Scientists and Their Discoveries, Tillis S. Pine and Joseph Levine, McGraw-Hill, New York, 1978.

Explains in simple language the discoveries and investigations of famous scientists including Galileo, Benjamin Franklin, Thomas Alva Edison, and Robert Goddard.

Solids & Liquids, David Glover, (in the Young Discoverers series), Kingfisher LKC (Larousse Kingfisher Chambers, Inc.), New York, 1993.
> Examines the composition and strength of materials, both solid and liquid, and features experiments, including chemical reactions.

Solids, Liquids and Gases, from the Ontario Science Centre, written by Louise Osborne and Carol Gold, Kids Can Press, Buffalo, New York, 1995.
> Uses experiments to illustrate concepts such as air pressure, condensation, and changes from liquids to solids and gases.

Solids, Liquids, and Gases: from Superconductors to the Ozone Layer, Melvin Berger, Putnam, New York, 1989.
> Discusses the nature, constitution, properties, and behavior of matter in its various solid, liquid, and gaseous forms.

What Is A Scientist?, Barbara Lehn, Millbrook, Brookfield, Connecticut, 1998.
> Simple text and photographs depict children engaged in various activities that make up the scientific process.

What Is The World Made Of?: All About Solids, Liquids, and Gases, Kathleen Weidner Zoehfeld, (in the Let's-Read-and-Find-Out Science series), HarperCollins, New York, 1998.
> In simple text, presents the three states of matter, solid, liquid, and gas, and describes their attributes.

Why Can't You Unscramble an Egg?: and Other Not Such Dumb Questions About Matter, Vicki Cobb, Lodestar Books, New York, 1990.
> Answers nine questions about matter, such as why does an ice cube float?, how much does air weigh?, how does wood burn? and other concepts about the nature of matter. Includes index.

Assessment Suggestions

Selected Student Outcomes

1. Students improve their ability to make objective observations and comparisons.

2. Students improve their ability to suggest explanations for phenomena.

3. Students are able to articulate a particulate theory of matter.

4. Students gain insight into the behavior of dry ice, phase change, and the kinetic molecular theory and can explain what happens to water ice and dry ice at the macroscopic and molecular levels when they are heated.

5. Students improve their ability to conduct an open-ended investigation in which they: choose a good investigable question, choose an appropriate kind of investigation to answer that question, plan and conduct a well-designed investigation, use careful reasoning to interpret their results, and are able to communicate about their investigation to others.

Built-In Assessment Activities

Scientific Journal. In Activities 1, 2, and 3, students have multiple opportunities to observe, compare, describe, and explain the nature of substances and phenomena. The teacher can use student work from the Scientific Journal (Notes from an Extraterrestrial, As if Seeing It for the First Time, Comparing Substances, Adding Energy, Dry Ice Explorations, Mystery of the Floating Bubbles, Marge's Systematic Observation, and Marge's Experiment Take 1 and 2) to assess students' abilities to make objective observations and comparisons, and their ability to suggest explanations for phenomena. (Outcomes 1, 2)

Energy and Matter. In Activity 2, students discuss, dispute, and observe models related to the particulate theory of matter and the kinetic molecular theory. The teacher can use the Energy and Matter Questionnaire as well as listen to small and large group discussion to assess what students' ideas are concerning both of these theories. (Outcomes 3, 4)

Open-Ended Investigations. In Activity 4, pairs of students conduct their own open-ended investigations. They (and the teacher) are provided with an Investigation Rubric with which to assess their investigations. The teacher can use the Investigation Rubric along with student work from the Scientific Journal (Planning Our Investigation, Our Dry Ice Investigation, and Follow-Up Investigation) as well as the presentations students make in Activity 4, Session 4: Sharing Results of Investigations to assess their growing abilities to investigate. (Outcomes 1, 2, 5)

Additional Assessment Ideas

Investigate Another Topic. Students can conduct an open-ended investigation related to a different topic or unit of study. The teacher can use the Investigation Rubric provided in this unit to assess the investigation and even compare to whether, with increased experience, students' investigation abilities improve. (Outcomes 1, 2, 5)

Design a Comic Strip. Students can make a comic strip in which they describe, explain, and illustrate what happens to dry ice and water ice as it is heated up. (Outcomes 3, 4)

The Royal Society Meets. The class can stage a meeting of the Royal Society of London at which distinguished members of the audience can argue and debate their ideas of how the molecular model of water ice would change when energy (heat) is added. Individual students can then write letters to Dalton to explain their ideas. (Outcomes 3, 4)

Inventive Applications. Students can be asked to design a machine or other useful invention involving dry ice and to explain how their design makes use of its special characteristics and properties. (Outcomes 1, 4)

Literature Connections

A Chilling Story: How Things Cool Down
by Eve and Albert Stwertka; illustrated by Mena Dolobowsky
Julian Messner/Simon and Schuster, New York. 1991
Grades: 4–8

How refrigeration and air conditioning work are simply explained, with sections on heat transfer, evaporation, and expansion. Humorous black and white drawings show a family and its cat testing out the principles in their home. The book provides nice examples of the practical applications of changing matter.

Everything Happens to Stuey
by Lilian Moore; illustrated by Mary Stevens
Random House, New York. 1960
Grades: 4–7

After smelling up the refrigerator with his secret formula, turning his sister's doll green with a magic cleaner, and having his invisible ink homework go awry, budding chemist Stuey is in trouble. In the end, he uses his knowledge to rescue his sister by fabricating a homemade flashlight. The illustrations, depiction of family life, and sex roles are dated, but the spirit of adventure is timeless.

June 29, 1999
by David Wiesner
Clarion Books, Houghton Mifflin, New York. 1992
Grades: 3–6

The science project of Holly Evans takes an extraordinary turn—or does it? This highly imaginative and humorous book has a central experimental component, and conveys the sense of unexpected results. Holly's planning, preparation, and analysis of her experiment provide a useful lesson.

The Lady Who Put Salt in Her Coffee
by Lucretia Hale
Harcourt, Brace Jovanovich, San Diego. 1989
Grades: K–6

When Mrs. Peterkin accidentally puts salt in her coffee, the entire family embarks on an elaborate quest to find someone to make it drinkable again. Visits to a chemist, an herbalist, and a wise woman result in a solution, but not without having tried some wild experiments first.

The Monster Garden
by Vivien Alcock
Delacorte Press, New York. 1988
Grades: 5–8

Frankie Stein, whose father is a genetic engineer, creates her own special monster, Monnie, from a "bit of goo" her brother steals from the lab. Scientific information is sprinkled throughout the book and Chapter 11 includes Frankie's experiment log. The book is a combination of fantasy, science fiction, and young adult novel with a strong female main character, an arrogant older brother, and a "friend" who spills the secret.

Susannah and the Poison Green Halloween
by Patricia Elmore; illustrated by Joel Schick
E.P. Dutton, New York. 1982
Grades: 5–7

Susannah and her friends try to figure out who put the poison in their Halloween candy when they trick-or-treated at the Eucalyptus Arms apartments. Tricky clues, changing main suspects, and some medical chemistry make this an exciting book, with lots of inference and mystery. The process Susannah and her friends go through to solve the mystery is very much like the scientific process.

Water's Way
by Lisa W. Peters; illustrated by Ted Rand
Arcade Publishing/Little Brown and Co., New York. 1991
Grades: K–3

"Water has a way of changing" inside and outside Tony's house, from clouds to steam to fog and other forms. Innovative illustrations show the changes in the weather outside while highlighting water changes inside the house. Although written for a younger audience, this book is useful for its clear description of the phase changes of water.

The Wise Woman and Her Secret
by Eve Merriam; illustrated by Linda Graves
Simon & Schuster, New York. 1991
Grades: K–4

A wise woman is sought out by many people for her wisdom. They look for the secret of her wisdom in the barn and in her house, but only little Jenny who lags and lingers and loiters and wanders finds it. The wise woman tells her, "...the secret of wisdom is to be curious—to take the time to look closely, to use all your senses to see and touch and taste and smell and hear. To keep on wandering and wondering." Though this book is intended for a younger reader, it is listed here because it emphasizes and values the role of curiosity, asking questions, and using all the senses when gathering data, and, as such, serves as a fine accompaniment to *Dry Ice Investigations*.

Summary Outlines

Activity 1: Scientist's Mindset

Session 1: Introduction to Observing

Getting Ready
1. Select mystery object.
2. Decide whether to use Scientific Journal or separate sheets.

Making Scientific Observations
1. Ask students to describe an object as if for first time.
2. Emphasize observations as what the senses can detect.
3. Distinguish between observations and other assumptions or inferences, and describe an object yourself with direct observations only. After students guess what it is, show it to them.

Introducing and Playing the Game
1. Explain game Notes from an Extraterrestrial. Students secretly choose object and describe it in writing, without using language that would identify it.
2. Students write their descriptions of the object they select.
3. In groups, students read descriptions out loud, as others guess. No one can guess until entire description of object has been read.
4. If there is time, have students play the game again.

Conclusion
1. Explain that the best scientists try to approach the world with fresh eyes, as an extraterrestrial might. Discoveries happen when a scientist notices something others overlooked or challenges an unvalidated assumption (e.g., Galileo and moons of Jupiter).
2. Tell students they should continue to make careful and objective observations throughout the unit, as they did in this session.
3. Have students write the name of the object they observed on their student sheet.

Session 2: Comparing Water Ice and Dry Ice

Getting Ready

Before the Day of the Activity
1. Plan how you will obtain dry ice.
2. Obtain a heat source for teacher demonstration.
3. Duplicate students sheets as needed.

On the Day of the Activity
1. Have materials ready.
2. Have Scientific Journals or student sheets on hand.

Immediately Before Class
1. Break dry ice into small pieces. Put one piece in cup for each group. Put cups in insulated container.
2. Put water ice cube in cup for each group.
3. Plug in hot plate or skillet.

Observing Water Ice Cubes
1. Tell students they will make observations of two objects, one they've seen often before, and one perhaps not. They should draw and write everything they can observe.
2. Distribute cup with ice to groups.
3. Have them record their observations.
4. After a few minutes, have class share observations.

Observing Dry Ice
1. Distribute cup with dry ice to groups.
2. Remind them not to touch the objects with their skin.
3. Have them observe and record as they did with first object.
4. After a few minutes, have class share observations.
5. If students mention "dry ice" or "carbon dioxide" say that there will be more information later on, and the main idea for now is to observe "as if for the first time."

Comparing and Contrasting
1. Ask students to continue their observations of both substances and record them.
2. After a few minutes, have one student from each group take both cups to a non-distracting location.
3. Ask students to share some of their comparisons.
4. Encourage students to write down questions they have.

Adding Heat
1. Gather the class for the demonstration.
2. Tell students you will place a water ice cube on the hot plate/skillet. What will happen? Ask them to observe carefully. Conduct demonstration, encourage observations, and, later, record them.
3. Encourage students to come up with their own explanations. Where did the ice go?
4. Tell students you will do the same with a piece of dry ice. Ask for predictions. Do the demonstration, encourage observations and comparisons, and then record them. (Make sure students do NOT touch the hot plate/skillet while it is hot.)
5. Begin a class list of observations and questions about dry ice.

Thinking Like a Scientist
1. Re-emphasize that students are now thinking as scientists do.
2. Write *"Nullius in verba"* on the board and explain its meaning.
3. Explain that they will have a chance to find out for themselves by making their own dry ice investigations.
4. Have students observe how the cups of water ice and dry ice have changed.

Session 3: Matter and Energy

Getting Ready

Before the Day of the Activity
1. Make the BB models.
2. Make needed transparencies.
3. Duplicate student sheets as needed.

On the Day of the Activity
1. Set up projector with transparencies and BB models nearby.
2. Have Scientific Journals or student sheets on hand.

Introduce a Particulate Model
1. Introduce John Dalton's idea that all matter is composed of tiny moving particles called atoms. Outline the history of this idea before Dalton.
2. Show Molecular Diagram of a Solid overhead. This gives a general idea of what scientists now think.

3. Summarize current knowledge—All matter is made of atoms, too small to be seen; atoms form molecules; there is space between molecules; molecules are always moving.
4. Explain that the diagram is a model—good for showing the physical arrangement, but does not show movement.
5. Show students the more dynamic BB model of a solid.
6. Explain that water is made of two hydrogen atoms and one oxygen atom and write formula on board. Do the same for carbon dioxide. They would look similar at the molecular level—the main difference would be the shape of the individual molecule.

What Happens When You Add Energy?

Part 1
1. Ask students what happened in previous session when heat energy was added to water ice and dry ice.
2. Project the Energy and Matter Questionnaire on overhead. The class will work in groups to figure out how the molecular model of water ice might change when energy is added.
3. Tell students they will read Part 1 and fill it out by themselves, then discuss their ideas in a group.
4. Distribute questionnaire or refer students to journals.
5. Have students start Part 1. Circulate among the groups to encourage discussion.
6. After 5–10 minutes, remind them that scientists engage in such discussions all the time. Also point out that changing one's mind can be the sign of an open thinker!
7. Ask several volunteers to explain their thinking about models A, B, C, or D. Keep discussion brief at this time.

Part 2
1. Explain that Part 2 lists three "true statements." Ask them to discuss and circle letter of model the statements best support.
2. Have them begin. Circulate, reminding them to consider the three statements as they discuss ideas.

Part 3
1. After 5–10 minutes have students go on to Part 3. Tell them not to change what they wrote in Part 1, but to check the box of the idea that now makes the most sense to them.
2. After students finish Part 3, again remind them that scientists do this kind of thinking and discussing all the time. Ask for a few volunteers to share their thinking.
3. Raise issues with all models to encourage students to confront old ideas and consider new ones. After discussion, explain that scientists have determined model C to be most accurate.

4. Use BB models to show what happens when energy is added to matter, first a solid, then liquid, then gas. Point out that the more energy added, the more energy (movement) the molecules have. With increased energy, molecules move faster and farther apart.

Temperature and Safety
1. Tell students they will work with dry ice in next session.
2. Draw a thermometer on the chalkboard and orient students to the temperature at which water freezes, and below, down to 110°F below zero (–79°C)—that's how cold dry ice is. Warn students it can "burn" their skin.
3. Say that dry ice can be harmful and that anyone who does not observe safety rules will not be allowed to participate.

Activity 2: Systematic Observation

Session 1: Exploring Dry Ice

Getting Ready

Before the Day of the Activity
1. Plan how you will obtain dry ice.
2. Obtain cold and hot water dispensers.
3. Acquire other needed materials.
4. Duplicate student sheets as needed. Copy Dry Ice Challenges sheet and cut into thirds.

On the Day of the Activity
1. Set up tray for each group with materials.
2. Have Scientific Journals or student sheets on hand.
3. Place trays of materials, straws, water dispensers, and dry ice in an insulated container in a central location.

Immediately Before Class
1. Fill and plug in water heater (or heat water for dispenser).
2. Break up dry ice and put pieces in an insulated container.

Seeking Explanations
1. Students will get to make their own discoveries in this session.
2. Say that, after initial excited reaction to a discovery, the next step is to come up with an explanation. Stress that no observation is too simple to say out loud, and no explanation "too stupid." They should stretch their mental muscles!

3. Say that, like scientists, they need to take time to write down their explanations and discuss them together.

Introducing the Materials
Briefly show students the materials and remind them again to record.

Starting the Dry Ice Explorations
1. Have a volunteer from each team get a tray.
2. Distribute journals (or student sheets).
3. Give small amount of dry ice to each group.
4. Circulate to assist as needed, visiting every team to encourage explanations.
5. After at least 10 minutes of free exploration, you may want to distribute the Dry Ice Challenges sheet.
6. Continue to circulate, asking questions, encouraging explanations, reminding students to record, and to observe safety rules.

Ending Explorations (for now)
1. Give 10-minute, then 5-minute, warning before stopping explorations.
2. Have students stop and clean up.
3. For homework, they should complete the Dry Ice Explorations sheets, focusing on writing four explanations for four things they tried or observed.

Session 2: Marge's Systematic Observation

Getting Ready

Before the Day of the Activity
1. Plan how to obtain dry ice.
2. Acquire remaining needed materials.
3. Make needed transparencies.
4. Duplicate student sheets as needed.
5. Write definitions for variable and systematic observation on butcher paper.

On the Day of the Activity
1. Set up trays for student groups.
2. Fill cups half full with water; add 6–8 drops dishwashing soap and stir.
3. Set up overhead, with transparencies and BB models nearby.
4. Have journals or separate sheets on hand.

Immediately Before Class
Break up dry ice and put in insulated container.

Sharing Explanations
1. Briefly discuss observations and explanations from previous session, using explorations sheet they did for homework.
2. Elicit several different explanations for same observation.
3. Add more questions to class list.

Introducing Systematic Observation
1. Write on board, "What happens when you put dry ice in soap solution?"
2. Ask for predictions. Write some on board.
3. Ask how class could find out. Ask if it matters how much dry ice is used, how much soap solution, when dry ice is added, what kind of container.
4. Explain that things that can vary are called variables. Post definition.
5. Scientists make a plan for all variables. Today the class will have one plan for all to follow. Show them the materials.
6. Say what they'll be doing is a more systematic way of observing. Define systematic observation and post.
7. After they conduct the systematic observation, they should record their observations and explanations.

Systematic Observation (or Marge Simpson's Hairdo!)
1. Distribute materials and journals (or student sheets) and have students begin.
2. Circulate, asking questions and reminding them to record observations and start discussing explanations.
3. When done, have students return materials and clean up.

Bubbling Up With Explanations
1. Facilitate a class discussion.
2. Ask questions to encourage thinking.
3. If students haven't mentioned it, introduce the idea that dry ice gives off a gas—the gas is what fills the bubbles.
4. Remind students of comparisons to water ice. Point out that dry ice is called "dry" because unlike frozen water ice it does not "melt" into a liquid but turns directly into a gas.

Introducing Phases and Phase Change
1. Show and discuss Phase Change Diagram A on overhead.
2. Do the same with Phase Change Diagram B.
3. Use all three BB models to go through the phases.
4. Do this several times. The last time emphasize the change from a solid to a gas—sublimation, which is what happens to dry ice.
5. If you planned to, distribute Phase Change Diagrams A and B for students to add to journals.

Session 3: The Mystery of the Floating Bubbles

Getting Ready

Before the Day of the Activity
1. Plan how to obtain dry ice.
2. Obtain an aquarium or similar container.
3. Acquire other needed materials and duplicate student sheets as needed.

On the Day of the Activity
1. Have journals or student sheets on hand.
2. Set out demonstration materials in central location.

Immediately Before Class
1. Break up dry ice and place in insulated container.
2. Put most of the cup of dry ice in the bottom of the aquarium.

Floating Bubbles Demonstration
1. Ask questions to review knowledge about dry ice.
2. Explain today's demonstration as another systematic observation.
3. You will blow a soap bubble and let it float down into the aquarium containing dry ice. Ask for predictions.
4. Blow bubbles above the aquarium, so bubbles will float down into it.
5. After several minutes of observing, ask for observations.
6. Distribute journals or student sheets and challenge students to come up with explanations.

Explaining the Mystery of the Floating Bubbles
1. Circulate as students discuss ideas.
2. When most students have completed the sheets, ask one to share their explanation and further questions that could help confirm the explanation. Write the explanation on the board.
3. Ask a group with a different explanation for their reasoning. Write it on the board. Ask for more explanations.
4. Lead a question-driven discussion to help explain the mystery.
5. Ask what evidence could be collected to help confirm that the bubble is floating on a layer of carbon dioxide gas.
6. Explain that carbon dioxide gas will not support a flame. Ask class for ideas on how the gas in the container could be identified.
7. Light a match and slowly lower it into the container.
8. Point out that making careful systematic observations often leads to more questions.
9. Add questions to class list.

Activity 3: Experimenting

Session 1: Marge's Experiments

Getting Ready

Before the Day of the Activity
1. Plan how to obtain dry ice.
2. Obtain hot and cold water dispensers.
3. Acquire remaining materials and duplicate student sheets as needed.
4. Write out definitions of experiment, test variable, and outcome variable on butcher paper.

On the Day of the Activity
1. Set up tray for each student group.
2. Add six drops of dishwashing soap to each cup.
3. Place water dispensers and dry ice in central location.
4. Have journals or student sheets on hand.

Immediately Before Class
1. Break up dry ice into pieces and place in insulated container.
2. Fill and plug in hot water heater (or heat water for dispenser).

Setting Up an Experiment
1. Remind students of the systematic observation they did to answer, "What happens when you put dry ice in soap solution?" Remind students of the definition of a systematic observation.
2. Today the question is, "Does temperature affect how fast dry ice turns to a gas?" (or "Does temperature affect the rate at which dry ice sublimates?"). Write the question on the board.
3. Ask for student ideas. While there are different ways to go about answering, the best ways compare two things that are alike in all ways except one. Ask what one thing should be different. [temperature]
4. Explain that this type of comparison is an experiment. All variables are kept the same except one; the one you vary is the test variable. Post definitions of experiment and test variable.
5. You need a carefully thought-out plan for an experiment. Today the class will all follow the same plan. Distribute Marge's Experiment: Take 1 or ask students to turn to it in their journals.

6. Present the plan, using props as needed. In the bottom of each of two cups are six drops of dishwashing soap. Same amount of water is added to each cup—one hot, one cold. Stir. At same time, add two similar-sized pieces of dry ice to each cup. Carefully observe and draw your own conclusion.

7. Summarize by saying all variables should be kept the same except temperature. Ask if students have questions about the procedure. Accept a few predictions about what might happen. Remind them to record their hypothesis, observations, conclusion, and explanation.

Conducting the Experiment
1. Have students obtain trays of materials.
2. After hot and cold water are added, walk around, providing dry ice.

Refining the Experiment
1. When all finish, ask original question, "Does temperature affect how fast dry ice turns to a gas?" Ask each group to explain how they knew.
2. Point out that groups based their conclusion on different indicators. Define outcome variable and post the definition. Ask for ideas about how it could be quantified.
3. They will now repeat the experiment, but try to find a quantitative way to compare or measure the outcome variable they use. Distribute Marge's Experiment: Take 2 or ask students to turn to it in their journals.
4. After hot and cold water are added, go around providing dry ice, checking to make sure group has come up with a way to quantitatively compare their results.
5. When students finish have them return materials and clean up.
6. Make list of several quantification methods students used. Discuss problems or surprises they encountered.

Activity 4: Conducting Dry Ice Investigations

Session 1: Choosing Investigable Questions

Getting Ready

Before the Day of the Activity
1. Make needed transparencies.
2. Cut Question Strips transparency into nine strips.
3. Duplicate student sheets as needed.
4. Cut set of Question Strips; put in envelope for each group of students.

5. Become familiar with Investigation Rubric.
6. Write definition of investigable question on butcher paper.

On the Day of the Activity
1. Set up overhead.
2. Have envelopes with Question Strips on hand, and both Sorting Questions sheets.
3. Have journals or student sheets on hand.

Introducing the Session
1. Focus on class list of questions about dry ice. Tell students they will be planning their own investigations.
2. First, they will consider what kinds of questions are needed for successful investigations.

Questions That Are Hard to Investigate
1. The first step is to come up with an investigable question— one that is able to be investigated. Post the definition.
2. Ask, "What might make a question hard to investigate?" [Not having the right equipment; too dangerous or impossible to do; something that is too big a question]
3. Though some of these kinds of questions are excellent, they are not possible to answer in a single classroom investigation.
4. Introduce the question sorting activity.

Categorizing Questions as Investigable or Not
1. Distribute envelopes with Question Strips and a Sorting Question 1 sheet. Students are to sort into "Investigable," "Not Investigable," and "Not Sure."
2. Put Sorting Questions 1 transparency on overhead with Question Strip transparencies.
3. When groups finish, ask one to share. Set their sort up on overhead and ask for their reasoning.
4. Ask for a show of hands of others who did it the same way. Ask for those who did it differently to explain their reasoning.
5. Continue process to arrive at sorting agreement. If necessary, bring to a close by stating that some categorizations are arguable, but scientists would most likely sort them this way. Place the final sort on overhead.

Generalizing About Investigable Questions
1. Ask students to organize their questions as on the overhead and then turn each strip over.
2. Help students generalize by discussing "measuring" questions, "what-happens-if" questions, and "comparison" questions (all investigable) and "how" and "why" questions (not investigable).

3. Explain that when students come up with a question, these criteria will be used to see if it is an investigable question.
4. Place Planning Our Investigation on the overhead and reveal #1, #2, and the first set of checking points.

Framing an Investigable Question
1. Focus students on overhead. To plan their investigation they first need to think about the general topic or situation they want to find out more about.
2. Then they will need to think of an investigable question, possible to answer through an experiment or a systematic observation.
3. Refer to class list of dry ice questions and have students brainstorm about some of these. Probably most will take some revising and focusing to become investigable.
4. Using questions suggested by the class, have students practice judging whether or not they are investigable.

Choosing an Investigation Pathway
1. Choosing what kind of investigation to do is just as important as choosing a good question.
2. Have students recall what a systematic observation and an experiment are.
3. Show Sorting Questions 2 transparency. This time they will sort strips into "best answered with a Systematic Observation," "best answered with an Experiment," or "Not Sure."
4. Categorize a few sample questions to give them the idea.
5. Distribute Sorting Questions 2 sheet and have students classify the five questions categorized as investigable into the three pathway categories.
6. Circulate, reminding students of definitions. Before they finish, prepare the overhead with the transparency and strips.
7. When students finish, ask one group to share their sort. Arrange the overhead in this way. Probe for reasoning. Invite others to share their sorts. Remind them that when a comparison is suggested, that is usually best answered with an experiment.
8. If class is able to agree on "correct" categorization, continue with the activity. If not, after allowing discussion, let them know that the exact categorization is arguable. A scientist would probably sort them in the way you now show on the overhead.

Generalizing About Appropriate Kinds of Investigations
1. Have students sort their questions in the same way then turn each strip over.
2. Ask students to generalize.
3. Point out that many kinds of questions can be changed to become comparison questions. Give an example.

4. When students choose what investigation method to use, you will evaluate according to the criteria the class has just discussed.

Choosing Their Topic and an Investigable Question
1. It is now time for groups to choose a topic, an investigable question, and whether it will be a systematic observation or an experiment.
2. You may want to point out that often people want to investigate something that will have a "whiz bang" effect. This was more appropriate for their earlier explorations—now their purpose should be to answer a question they have about dry ice.
3. Have students turn to Planning Our Investigation sheet in journals, or distribute student sheet. Have them fill out the first page. Meanwhile, distribute copies of the Systematic Observation or Experiment? sheet or have students turn to it in their journals.
4. Circulate, providing guidance as needed.
5. As groups finish, they can trade questions with each other and critique using checking points.
6. In the next session, they will design their own investigation plan.

Session 2: Making an Investigation Plan

Getting Ready

Before the Day of the Activity
Duplicate student sheets as needed.

On the Day of the Activity
Have journals or student sheets on hand.

Planning their Investigations
1. Remind students of last session.
2. In this session, they will complete their planning.
3. They are to complete appropriate pages of Planning Our Investigation, depending on whether they are doing an experiment or systematic observation.
4. Tell students you will distribute Materials Lists for them to complete.
5. Have students complete the sheets. Circulate, offering guidance as needed.
6. As groups finish, distribute and have students complete the first page of Our Dry Ice Investigation sheet. Collect the Materials List sheets.
7. Decide on your method of feedback on investigation plans.

Session 3: Conducting Investigations

Getting Ready

Before the Day of the Activity
1. Plan how to obtain dry ice.
2. Make transparency of Investigation Rubric.
3. Review Materials Lists.
4. Acquire remaining materials needed.
5. Duplicate student sheets as needed.

On the Day of the Activity
1. Place materials students requested in central location.
2. Set out a stack of trays for students to use for transport.
3. Set up overhead.
4. Have journals or student sheets on hand.

Immediately Before Class
Break up dry ice into pieces and place in insulated container.

Conducting Investigations
1. Class can now carry out the investigations they've planned!
2. Tell students where materials are, and state any related rules.
3. Remind students to fill out second page of Our Dry Ice Investigation student sheet.
4. Project Investigation Rubric on overhead.
5. Tell students that if they finish 15 minutes or more before end of session and want to refine and repeat the experiment, they can, or they can conduct a related additional investigation.
6. Have students begin their investigations.
7. If students do have time for follow-up investigations, remind them to fill out a sheet for each one.
8. When students finish, have them take materials to a central location according to your clean up instructions.

Session 4: Sharing Results of Investigations

Getting Ready
1. Choose how to structure the session.
2. Acquire any needed materials.

Sharing Results
Options include:
       Poster Session
       Sentence Strip Bonanza
       Peer Review
       Publishing Their Results
       Oral Reports

SCIENTIFIC JOURNAL

Dry Ice
Investigations

FOR GRADES 5–9

Name _____

Name _____

Notes from an Extraterrestrial

Object 1 _____

_____

_____

_____

_____

_____

_____

_____

_____

Object 2 _____

_____

_____

_____

_____

_____

_____

_____

_____

© 1999 by The Regents of the University of California, LHS-GEMS. *Dry Ice Investigations.* **May be duplicated for classroom use.**

Name _____

As if Seeing It for the First Time

Observations of Substance #1:
(Draw and describe what you observe.)

1. _____   6. _____

2. _____   7. _____

3. _____   8. _____

4. _____   9. _____

5. _____   10. _____

Observations of Substance #2:
(Draw and describe what you observe.)

1. _____   6. _____

2. _____   7. _____

3. _____   8. _____

4. _____   9. _____

5. _____   10. _____

© 1999 by The Regents of the University of California, LHS-GEMS. *Dry Ice Investigations.* **May be duplicated for classroom use.**

Name _____

Comparing Substances

Ways that water ice and dry ice are similar:

1. _____

2. _____

3. _____

4. _____

5. _____

6. _____

7. _____

8. _____

9. _____

10. _____

Ways that water ice and dry ice are different:

1. _____

2. _____

3. _____

4. _____

5. _____

6. _____

7. _____

8. _____

9. _____

10. _____

© 1999 by The Regents of the University of California, LHS-GEMS. *Dry Ice Investigations.* **May be duplicated for classroom use.**

Name _____

Adding Energy

Adding energy to water ice—observations:
(Draw and describe what you observe.)

1. _____   6. _____
2. _____   7. _____
3. _____   8. _____
4. _____   9. _____
5. _____   10. _____

Adding energy to dry ice—observations:
(Draw and describe what you observe.)

1. _____   6. _____
2. _____   7. _____
3. _____   8. _____
4. _____   9. _____
5. _____   10. _____

© 1999 by The Regents of the University of California, LHS-GEMS. *Dry Ice Investigations.* **May be duplicated for classroom use.**

Name _____

Energy and Matter Questionnaire

© 1999 by The Regents of the University of California, LHS-GEMS. *Dry Ice Investigations.* **May be duplicated for classroom use.**

Part 1 How would the molecular model of "water ice" change when energy (heat) is added? Check the box of the statement that you think is most accurate.

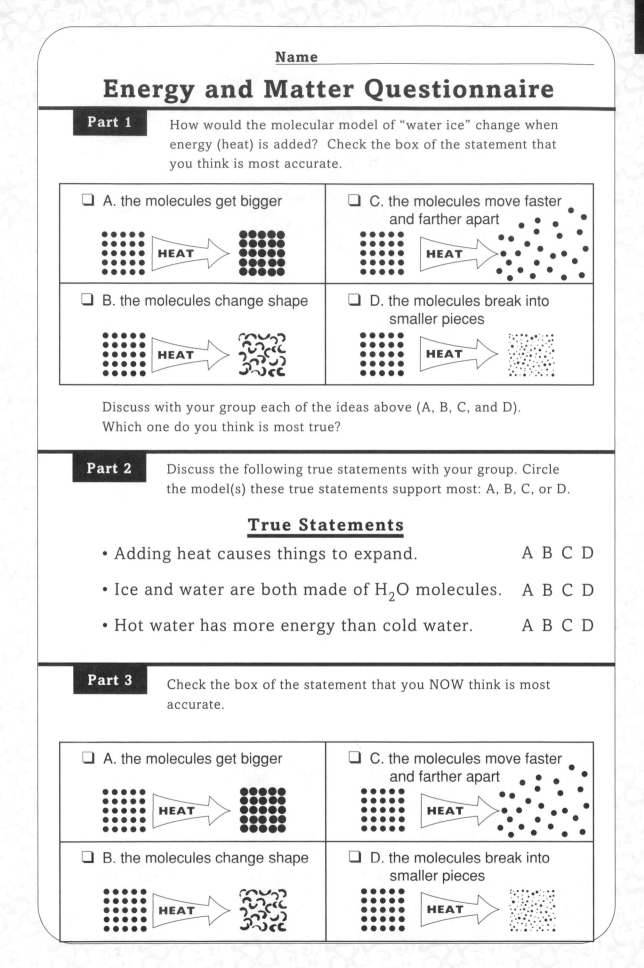

☐ A. the molecules get bigger

HEAT

☐ C. the molecules move faster and farther apart

HEAT

☐ B. the molecules change shape

HEAT

☐ D. the molecules break into smaller pieces

HEAT

Discuss with your group each of the ideas above (A, B, C, and D). Which one do you think is most true?

Part 2 Discuss the following true statements with your group. Circle the model(s) these true statements support most: A, B, C, or D.

True Statements

• Adding heat causes things to expand. A B C D

• Ice and water are both made of H_2O molecules. A B C D

• Hot water has more energy than cold water. A B C D

Part 3 Check the box of the statement that you NOW think is most accurate.

☐ A. the molecules get bigger

HEAT

☐ C. the molecules move faster and farther apart

HEAT

☐ B. the molecules change shape

HEAT

☐ D. the molecules break into smaller pieces

HEAT

© 1999 by The Regents of the University of California, LHS-GEMS. *Dry Ice Investigations.* **May be duplicated for classroom use.**

Team Members: _____

_____

Dry Ice Explorations

Exploration #1:

- What You Did
(Use words and drawings to show what you did.)

- What You Observed
(Use words and drawings to communicate what you observed.)

- Your Explanation
(How can you explain the results?)

Team Members: _____

_____

Dry Ice Explorations

Exploration #2:

- What You Did
(Use words and drawings to show what you did.)

- What You Observed
(Use words and drawings to communicate what you observed.)

- Your Explanation
(How can you explain the results?)

© 1999 by The Regents of the University of California, LHS-GEMS. *Dry Ice Investigations.* **May be duplicated for classroom use.**

© 1999 by The Regents of the University of California, LHS-GEMS. *Dry Ice Investigations.* **May be duplicated for classroom use.**

Team Members: _____

_____

Dry Ice Explorations

Exploration #3:

- What You Did
(Use words and drawings to show what you did.)

- What You Observed
(Use words and drawings to communicate what you observed.)

- Your Explanation
(How can you explain the results?)

© 1999 by The Regents of the University of California, LHS-GEMS. *Dry Ice Investigations.* **May be duplicated for classroom use.**

Team Members: _____

_____

Dry Ice Explorations

Exploration #4:

- What You Did
(Use words and drawings to show what you did.)

- What You Observed
(Use words and drawings to communicate what you observed.)

- Your Explanation
(How can you explain the results?)

© 1999 by The Regents of the University of California, LHS-GEMS. *Dry Ice Investigations.* **May be duplicated for classroom use.**

Team Members: _____

_____

Marge's Systematic Observation

Question: What happens when you put dry ice in soap solution?

Prediction (What do you think will happen?):

Procedure/Plan:

What You Observed:

Your Conclusion (What do the results tell you? Are they the same as your prediction or not?):

Your Explanation (How can you explain the results?):

Team Members: _____

_____

Mystery of the Floating Bubbles

1) Draw what you observed:

2) What do you think explains why the bubbles are floating?

3) What new questions do you have that would help you test your explanation?

© 1999 by The Regents of the University of California, LHS-GEMS. *Dry Ice Investigations.* **May be duplicated for classroom use.**

Team Members: _____

_____

Marge's Experiment: Take 1

Question: Does temperature affect how fast dry ice turns to a gas?

Hypothesis:

Procedure/Plan:

- Put 6 drops of soap in the bottom of two cups.

- Add hot water to one cup.

- Add the same amount of cold water to the second cup.

- Stir each water/soap mixture.

- Get two similar-sized chunks of dry ice.

- Add one to each cup, at the same time.

The Results (What you observed!):

Conclusion (What do the results tell you?
        Were the results the same as your hypothesis or not?):

Explanation (How can you explain the results?):

© 1999 by The Regents of the University of California, LHS-GEMS. *Dry Ice Investigations.* **May be duplicated for classroom use.**

© 1999 by The Regents of the University of California, LHS-GEMS. *Dry Ice Investigations.* May be duplicated for classroom use.

Team Members: _____

_____

Marge's Experiment: Take 2

Question: Does temperature affect how fast dry ice turns to a gas?

Outcome variable (The result that you want to quantify.):

Hypothesis: (State how the outcome variable will be different.):

Procedure/Plan:

- Put 6 drops of soap in the bottom of two cups.

- Add hot water to one cup.

- Add the same amount of cold water to the second cup.

- Stir each water/soap mixture.

- Get two similar-sized chunks of dry ice.

- Add one to each cup, at the same time.

The Results (What you observed! Compare the outcome variable in each cup.):

Conclusion (What do the results tell you?
Were the results the same as your hypothesis or not?
Did having a way to measure results give a more precise answer
to the question?):

Explanation (How can you explain the results?):

Team Members: _____

_____

Planning Our Investigation

1. We are interested in finding out more about: _____

_____

2. Our investigable question is: _____

_____

_____

_____

Checking Points:

There is a good investigable question:

❏ Uses available equipment and materials.

❏ Is safe and realistic.

❏ Can be answered with a single investigation (*not* too big a question).

❏ Is a "measuring" question, a "what-happens-if" question, or a "comparison" question (*not* a "how" or "why" question).

3. The approach we are taking in our investigation is:

❏ conducting a systematic observation (setting up a situation according to a plan and then carefully observing it over time)

❏ conducting an experiment (comparing two or more situations where all variables are the same but one)

Checking Points:

An appropriate kind of investigation was selected:

❏ Decided to do a systematic observation because a "measuring" or "what-happens-if" question was chosen.

or

❏ Decided to do an experiment because a "comparison" question was chosen or because we turned another kind of question into a "comparison" question.

© 1999 by The Regents of the University of California, LHS-GEMS. *Dry Ice Investigations*. **May be duplicated for classroom use.**

© 1999 by The Regents of the University of California, LHS-GEMS. *Dry Ice Investigations.* **May be duplicated for classroom use.**

If you are conducting a **systematic observation**, please think through the following questions:

Things to decide (planning the conditions in the situation): _____

_____

_____

_____

_____

_____

_____

Possible results (outcome variables): _____

_____

_____

_____

_____

Say if (and how) you plan to quantify the outcome: _____

_____

_____

_____

_____

If you are conducting an **experiment**, please think through the following questions:

Things to be changed (test variable): _____
_____
_____
_____

Things to stay the same (controlled variables): _____
_____
_____
_____
_____

Result to be looked at (outcome variable): _____
_____
_____
_____
_____

Say if (and how) you plan to quantify the outcome: _____
_____
_____
_____
_____

© 1999 by The Regents of the University of California, LHS-GEMS. *Dry Ice Investigations.* **May be duplicated for classroom use.**

© 1999 by The Regents of the University of California, LHS-GEMS. *Dry Ice Investigations*. **May be duplicated for classroom use.**

page 4

Describe a plan for your systematic observation/experiment that takes all of these conditions and variables into account (use words and drawings):

Checking Points:

The investigation is well designed:

For Systematic Observations:

❏ Planned the conditions (variables).

❏ Identified possible outcome variables.

❏ Have clear and careful procedure that takes variables into account.

For Experiments:

❏ Identified test variable.

❏ Controlled variables.

❏ Identified outcome variable.

❏ Have clear and careful procedure that takes variables into account.

Systematic Observation or Experiment?

In a *systematic observation*, you make a plan, decide on the conditions, follow the plan, and then carefully observe what happens over time.

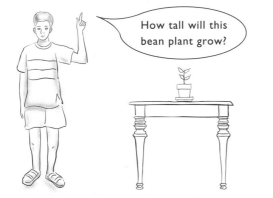

> How tall will this bean plant grow?

Plan:
1. Plant bean in soil.
2. Put near window.
3. Water once per day.
4. Measure height after 3 weeks.

In an *experiment*, you make a comparison between two (or more) situations, keeping all things the same except one.

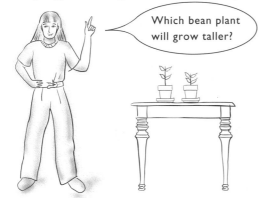

> Which bean plant will grow taller?

Things to keep the same:
- size of container
- amount of soil
- amount of sun
- amount of water

A *test variable* is the one thing you plan to be different in an experiment. You decide on what is going to be different *before* doing the experiment.

The kind of bean

An *outcome variable* is the result you compare in an experiment. You don't know what you will find out until *after* you do the experiment.

The height of the plants

© 1999 by The Regents of the University of California, LHS-GEMS. Dry Ice Investigations. **May be duplicated for classroom use.**

© 1999 by The Regents of the University of California, LHS-GEMS. *Dry Ice Investigations.* **May be duplicated for classroom use.**

Team Members: _____

_____

Our Dry Ice Investigation

Question (This is the question your investigation will try to answer.):

Hypothesis:

Procedure/Plan (What materials will you need? Describe each step of the procedure. Draw and write out all you plan to do.):

Check one:

❑ this is a systematic observation (we have set up the conditions)

❑ this is an experiment (we have controlled the variables in our two comparison groups)

© 1999 by The Regents of the University of California, LHS-GEMS. *Dry Ice Investigations.* **May be duplicated for classroom use.**

Our Dry Ice Investigation (continued)

Results (What happened? What did you observe? Be very clear and precise. If you quantified the outcome, share that information here.):

Conclusion (What do the results tell you? Were the results the same as your hypothesis or not?):

Explanation (How can you explain the results?):

Problems (Were there any problems? What might you do differently if you did the test again?):

More Questions (Did the test make you think of more questions?):

Team Members: _____

Follow-Up Investigation

Our first Investigation Question was:

The follow-up question we want to investigate is:

Hypothesis:

Procedure/Plan (Describe each step of the procedure. Draw and write out all you plan to do.):

Results (What happened? What did you observe? Be very clear and precise. If you quantified the outcome, share that information here.):

Conclusion (What do the results tell you? Were the results the same as your hypothesis or not?):

Explanation (How can you explain the results?):

© 1999 by The Regents of the University of California, LHS-GEMS. *Dry Ice Investigations.* **May be duplicated for classroom use.**

Dry Ice Rap *by LB*

My name's dry ice
Don't ask me why
I am not ice
Though I guess I'm dry
It's true I'm cold
So chill I burn
If you check me out
There's lots to learn
All sorts of stuff
To investigate
I'll let you watch me
Sublimate!

Call me CO_2
But know the rules
Handle me with care
Use glove or tools
Place me in
A plastic sack
See that ziplock
Blow its stack
Don't breathe me in
Or play the fool
My name's dry ice
And I'm way cool!

202